England in crisis 1640–60

David Sharp

Series Editors
Martin Collier
Erica Lewis
Rosemary Rees

D0549985

HEINEMANN ADVANCED HISTORY

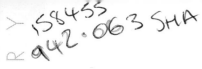

Heinemann is an imprint of Pearson Education Limited, a company incorporated in England and Wales, having its registered ocffice at Edinburgh Gate, Harlow, Essex, CM20 2JE.
Registered company number: 872828
Heinemann is a registered trademark of Pearson Education Limited

OXFORD MELBOURNE AUCKLAND
JOHANNESBURG BLANTYRE GABORONE
IBADAN PORTSMOUTH NH (USA) CHICAGO

© Heinemann Educational Publishers 2000

First published 2000

ISBN 978 0 435 32714 9

09
10 9 8 7

Typeset by Wyvern 21 Ltd

Printed and bound in China (CTPS/07)

Picture research by Ginny Stroud-Lewis

Photographic acknowledgements
The author and publisher would like to thank the following for permission to reproduce photographs:

Trustees of the British Museum: 113; Fotomas Index/Barnaby's Picture Library: 4, 7, 10, 17, 20, 24, 45, 48, 57, 71, 114, 116 (top and bottom), 120; Fotomas: 108; Heselrige Collection, Leicestershire Museum: 109; Hulton Getty: 59; Mansell Collection: 27; Mary Evans Picture Library: 16, 18, 29, 36, 38, 40, 43, 46, 66, 70, 117, 125, 129, 130, 168, 173; National Portrait Gallery: 35; The Royal Armouries: 47

Cover photograph: C M Dixon

CONTENTS

Part 3: The Restoration

HOW TO USE THIS BOOK

This book is divided into three parts, each containing AS chapters and A2 sections. The AS chapters explain what happened in England between 1640 and 1660, with a brief introduction giving the background to this period. The text gives the student in-depth information and some analysis.

The summary questions which appear at the end of the AS chapters will challenge the student to use the information to analyse, grasp priorities and explain important aspects of the subject. It is hoped that they will acquire a clear understanding of the key features of each topic.

The A2 sections are designed to pose the leading questions about the period, and provide some guidance with regard to the debates about these questions. They also contain some more detail. It is hoped that the A2 sections are written in such a way that they will be useful for AS students who wish to extend their understanding of the period.

At the end of each part there is an assessment section. These have been based on the requirements of the new AS and A2 specifications. There is guidance in the assessment sections on how students might answer the questions.

PART 1: THE CIVIL WAR

INTRODUCTION

The Civil War and its aftermath 1640–9

In 1640 Charles I, having tried to rule England without a Parliament, was forced to call one as a result of a successful revolt by his Scottish subjects. This Parliament, already suspicious of his policies in both politics and religion, took the opportunity to reverse some of his measures during the years of the Personal Rule (1629–40), and to destroy some of his hated advisers. There was, however, no agreement between Charles and the majority of Parliament and by 1642 they had drifted into a state of mutual mistrust.

Charles, determined to resist any further attacks on royal powers, went to war with Parliament in the summer of 1642. No one had really wanted this war and most expected it to be short. In the event, it lasted until 1646, cost the lives of thousands and left the country confused and on the verge of anarchy. New and increasingly radical ideas had emerged during the war with some members of the 'lower orders' wanting to 'have a say' in whatever settlement there was. Unlike the gentlemen of Parliament, they hoped for real political change, with more rights for those who, before the war, had no real say in politics. Their 'power base' was the Parliamentary army that, in 1647, revolted against Parliament and tried to negotiate directly with the King. Charles, seeing his enemies in confusion, started another war in 1648. When he was defeated, the army and some MPs decided to try him as 'an enemy of the people' and a war criminal. Because the army had control by then, this minority had their way and Charles was executed on 30 January 1649. England became a republic for the only time in its history.

There has been a lot of historical debate about the causes and consequences of the events of 1640–9, and the debates continue. No one historian can claim to have all the information, nor all the answers.

AS: NARRATIVE AND EXPLANATION

CHAPTER 1

The background to crisis, 1629–40

INTRODUCTION

In 1629 Charles I had dismissed Parliament, after a series of parliaments which had proved to be uncooperative towards him. He forbade people to 'speak of calling another'. During the next eleven years Charles ruled without Parliament – the Personal Rule or, as some called it, 'the Eleven Years Tyranny'. Europe was gripped in a great war, the Thirty Years War, and to some observers England seemed peaceful in comparison with the devastation in Germany. Under the surface, however, there were problems gathering.

CHARLES I, 1625–49

Personality and character

- Like his father James, Charles was a believer in the **divine right of kings**. Unlike his father, he actually tried to put it into practice.
- He saw all criticism, all discussion, as being potentially treacherous. He regarded anyone who questioned his actions as being disloyal.
- He was a poor communicator; his speeches in Parliament were brief and they often took the form of attacks on Parliament, or statements of his views about which he would allow no argument.
- Given his belief in the divine right of kings, he saw all Parliament's privileges, or rights, as being subject to the approval of the sovereign (the king), not as liberties which had existed independent of the sovereign's wishes.

Charles I.

- He was, in some ways, shy and tended to have only a small circle of friends or courtiers. He was deeply attached to his minister Buckingham until his assassination in 1628. He then transferred his affections to his wife Henrietta Maria, a French princess who had a considerable influence over him. She was a strong 'absolutist', who was brought up in the continental belief that the monarch was all powerful. She hated parliaments and the idea that subjects had 'liberties' which monarchs could not interfere with.

England in crisis 1640–60

- In religion, he favoured the High Church Arminian group within the Church of England, because they stressed the God-like nature of the king. This group, hated by the **Puritan** majority of the Church of England, believed that ceremonies, statues and bowing at the name of Jesus were vital parts of church services. To Puritans, this seemed like a return to the Roman Catholic services.
- Charles had a rigid mind that found it hard to adjust to new situations, or to compromise.
- He could be devious and dishonest but, as he thought he had only to justify his actions to himself, he never actually realised this.

In the 1630s, with no Parliament sitting, Charles and his leading advisers pursued policies that the majority of the **political nation** found very disturbing.

RELIGION

England was a strongly Protestant country but within English Protestantism there were differing views about how the Anglican Church of England, which everyone had to attend on a Sunday, should be run.

- **Puritans.** Many Anglicans of strong views wanted few ceremonies in Church, and no statues or paintings. According to their views, the minister should not be dressed in robes, and the minister's main function was to preach. These 'Puritans' were probably in a majority.
- **Presbyterians.** Some Puritans went even further and wanted no bishops – just 'elders' elected by a church council. They were known as Presbyterians.
- **Independents.** Some even more extreme Puritans, called Independents, wanted to elect their own ministers and wanted only a very loose church organisation.

The Church of England had managed to accommodate most of the Puritans within it by being a broad, tolerant church. Most English people, however, were very intolerant towards Roman Catholics. The hatred and fear of Roman Catholicism was to be one of the main elements in the crisis of 1640–2.

Anti-Catholicism

This was one of the strongest forces in English life in the seventeenth century. For most English people, Catholicism was associated with the burnings of Protestants under Mary, with massacres of Protestants abroad (of course, Protestants had also massacred Catholics) and, above all, with England's traditional enemies Spain and France. The aim of the Spanish Armada of 1588 had been the reconversion, by force, of England to Catholicism. English Protestants looked to the continent where absolute monarchs saw Catholicism as part of their authoritarian system. This seemed at odds with the idea of English liberty. Also English Catholics were seen as dangerous because their first loyalty, in theory, was to the Pope, 'a foreign prince', not to the English sovereign. Catholicism was therefore seen as unpatriotic, religiously evil, and the driving force behind England's enemies. Anti-Catholic attitudes were deeply rooted in English society from the top to the bottom and could unite people in a way that nothing else could. The **Gunpowder Plot of 1605**, of course, only served to confirm this prejudice in the public mind.

Charles's religious policies in the 1630s and Archbishop Laud

Charles favoured a group within the Church of England called Arminians, led by William Laud, who had a lot of control over the Church even before he became Archbishop of Canterbury in 1633. As head of the Church of England, the monarch could, if he or she wished, change its direction and services. Charles supported the Arminian group and Laud became one of his closest advisers. **Laud's beliefs** and policies for the Church were to be one of the main reasons for the breakdown of 1640.

Laud's changes. Laud was determined to force his views on the previously 'broad' Anglican Church that had contained bishops and ministers of varying degrees of Puritanism and Protestantism. His measures were carried out by enforcing discipline whatever resistance there might be – a policy which became known as 'thorough'. The Laudian changes to the Church of England, with their Roman Catholic-looking ceremonies, aroused the greatest suspicion. It seemed to many that Laud was bringing in Roman

KEY TERM

The Gunpowder Plot 1605 was an attempt by a group of Catholics led by Robert Catesby and Guy Fawkes to blow up James I in the Houses of Parliament.

KEY THEME

The beliefs of Laud Laud believed in 'the beauty of holiness' – that images, priests, garments, statues and more ceremony should be used. He hoped to make the Church as powerful politically as it had been before the Reformation under Henry VIII. He was also a firm supporter of the divine right of kings.

Catholicism by the back door. Those who were worried about Charles's Personal Rule, seeing it as a possible attempt to set up an absolutist monarchy on the European model, saw Laud as an agent of these policies because of his firm support for divine right.

CHARLES'S FINANCIAL POLICIES

During the 1630s, Charles had to raise money. With no Parliament to vote him subsidies (taxation based on the value of the subject's goods), he had to find new sources of revenue. Many of these were regarded as illegal by the legally-minded **gentry**.

- He fined those who had built outside the city walls of London.
- He declared large areas of England royal forests and fined all those who lived there as trespassers; he also fined those who refused knighthoods.
- The most worrying of Charles's money-raising schemes was 'ship money' where all had to pay to maintain the Royal Navy. Ship money had been raised in the past but only from coastal counties and only in emergencies. Charles collected it every year from 1634 onwards and it seemed to become a regular tax that was not laid down in the constitution.
- It seemed to many that Charles and his ministers were creating new taxes, or reviving ones long dead, so that he could be independent of Parliament. If he could raise enough money, Parliament would never meet again and Charles could set up an absolutist rule.

THE COURT

Charles's Court was regarded with suspicion by the country gentry. Both Elizabeth and James had encouraged the country gentlemen to come to Court and made efforts to meet them. Charles had no wish to do so. His Court was a 'closed' one – only a small inner circle of advisers and courtiers. His French wife Henrietta Maria, who was Roman Catholic, did as much as she could to convert

Archbishop Laud.

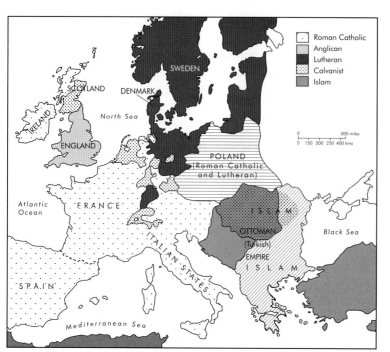

Europe in the early seventeenth century.

courtiers to Catholicism. She also had her own chapel built. The Court gained the reputation of being a small group of Catholic sympathisers, leading Charles astray.

FOREIGN POLICY

In the 1630s England was neutral in what the gentry regarded as the 'great religious war' between the Catholics and the Protestants which had raged since 1618 (the Thirty Years War).

• The sympathies of much of the 'political nation' were with the Protestant cause and the country gentry would have liked to see England support the German Protestant princes, the Protestant Dutch Republic (the United Provinces) and the Swedes.
• In fact, Charles had more sympathy for the leading Catholic power: Spain. Spain was, for the average English country gentleman, the constant enemy of England. Charles actually allowed the Spanish to land troops in England to rest on their way from Spain to the Spanish Netherlands. He also tried to use the fleet built

with ship money to protect the Spanish treasure ships against attacks by the Dutch.

THE SCOTTISH CRISIS

Personal Rule, however unpopular with the majority of the 'political nation', collapsed not because of resistance in England, but in Charles's Scottish kingdom. It is an open question whether Charles could have continued to rule without Parliament had he not been overcome by the Scottish crisis, a crisis of his own making. However, what is certain is that events in **Scotland** shaped events in England between 1637 and 1640.

Scottish concerns. Charles had already aroused deep resentment and suspicion amongst the Scottish nobles. This was because of a number of issues.

- **Land and the Act of Revocation.** In 1625 Charles had issued an Act of Revocation cancelling all grants of royal land and church land made since 1540. This affected many Scottish landowners, who were unsure if they would be allowed to keep land that they legally thought was theirs. Church land was an issue that spilt over into religion. Not only did the landowners see themselves as rightful owners of land that had once belonged to the Roman Catholic Church which had been swept away but, if church land returned to the Church, it could be the first step towards creating a rich, strong Church again on the Roman Catholic model. Also, the Act of Revocation sent shivers down the spines of English gentry who had acquired church lands in the past one hundred years. They were worried that Charles might find some legal device to do the same in England. Certainly Laud would have welcomed such a move.
- **Laudianism and the New Prayer Book.** Charles's coronation as King of Scotland in Edinburgh in 1633 was conducted with High Church Laudian ceremony. This offended the prejudices of the Scots. Laud was determined to bring the Scottish Church into line with what was happening to the English Church. In 1636 he issued new canons (instructions on the conduct of services), by royal

Scotland Charles was also, of course, King of Scotland and Scotland was a separate kingdom. It was more feudal, with the great landowners and clan chiefs able to command the obedience of a large part of its population. Scotland was also a more Protestant country, especially in the lowlands. The Scottish bishops had always kept down ceremonies because of the deeply-held views of Scottish Puritans. Many Scots were in any case Presbyterian, which was an extreme form of Protestantism. The combination of an independent-minded population, an absentee king, and Presbyterianism was to be an explosive one. When Charles decided to enforce Laudianism on the Scottish people he met fierce resistance.

proclamation, without reference to the General
Assembly of the Scottish Church. In 1637 a version of
the new 1633 English **Prayer Book** was introduced. It
proved to be a spark that set Scotland aflame.

- **The Scottish National Covenant, 1638.** In February 1638
  the Scottish National Covenant was drawn up. It rejected
  the canons and the Prayer Book and opened the way to
  full Presbyterianism. However, it was left vague enough
  for nearly everybody to sign as it did not state that the
  Covenanters (as those who signed were known) wanted
  to get rid of bishops. To Charles, the Covenant spelt
  open rebellion. Although Charles seemed to be prepared
  to negotiate with the Scottish Covenanters, in fact he
  was stringing them along while he prepared for war.

Scotland prepares. The Scots, despite Charles's negotiations,
became more determined. In November 1638 the Scottish
National Assembly abolished High Commission (the
highest Church court) and removed the bishops. They also
started to collect an army, well aware that Charles was
doing the same. The difference was that the Scottish army
had a good percentage of professional Scottish soldiers who
had been fighting in the Thirty Years War.

Weaknesses in the English army. Charles's forces were
quite different.

- As early as 1628 Charles had called for a 'perfect militia'
  but as this was to be paid for by local taxes the actual
  equipment and training of the **militia** were of poor
  quality. Most militiamen had never fired their weapons.
  The Cambridgeshire militia, for example, had the wrong
  calibre musket balls for their weapons and half the pikes
  were useless as the heads had fallen off the rotten poles.
- Professional soldiers, 'muster masters', were supposed to
  train the militia but counties often refused to pay their
  salaries so they drifted off. The gentry, if they did have
  any interest in the militia, were not prepared to take
  advice from 'low-born' soldiers. They commanded their
  militia companies largely for the status it gave them in
  country society, not because they were interested in
  creating a well-oiled military machine.

The new Prayer Book
Congregations in Scotland
rioted at the reading of the
new Prayer Book. One bishop
had to conduct services with
loaded pistols in the pulpit.
There was a famous incident
in St Giles Cathedral in
Edinburgh when a woman
shouting 'the mass has come
amongst us' hurled her stool
in disgust. Her attitude
summed up majority opinion.

The Earl of Arundel.

KEY THEME

The militia and military failure In theory, in England and Wales every able-bodied adult male was to help in the defence of the country. In practice, groups were selected for very basic military training, usually twice a year at 'musters'. The militia tended to be amateur and ill-trained – no match for professional soldiers.

The ill-discipline and incompetence of the majority of the militia is not a minor point.

Firstly, given Charles's grand plans for a perfect militia it shows the gap between the appearance and reality of Personal Rule. Without the wholehearted cooperation of the local gentry, Charles could not create a viable military force, one of the most important elements in a powerful independent monarchy.

Secondly, had the militia been efficient Charles might have won the Bishops' Wars, or at least not suffered the humiliating defeats that led directly to the crisis of 1640.

- The rank and file were usually poor soldiers, who disliked marching out of their own districts and deserted in large numbers. Many had sympathy for the Scots who were seen as fellow sufferers. Few wanted to fight for the hated Laudian Prayer Book.

The First Bishops' War, 1639. In 1639 Charles spent £185,000 on military operations, while his commander, the Earl of Arundel, found himself unable to launch a successful offensive. Arundel did not improve matters by riding to meet his troops in a coach lent by the papal nuncio (the Pope's ambassador in England) with the Pope's coat of arms on the doors. This only confirmed the idea that this was a Catholic war against honest Protestants. Once again Charles, his advisers and ministers misunderstood public opinion. To try to improve matters Thomas Wentworth, Earl of Strafford, was recalled from Ireland but he could not retrieve the situation. In these circumstances Strafford, perhaps out of touch with English affairs having been so long in Ireland, advised the King to call a Parliament. He expected, in this crisis, that traditional loyalty to the Crown would reassert itself and a Parliament would vote money for an offensive to crush the Scottish rebellion. The City of London had a poor relationship with Charles and was not prepared to lend him money, so Charles had few options.

- His military costs were estimated at £600,000 for 1640 and his high-handed treatment of the City of London proved short-sighted when a request for a loan of £100,000 was rejected and a £10,000 gift offered instead.
- He did not call Parliament because he had suddenly been converted to the idea of partnership between Crown and Parliament. Neither had he seen Personal Rule as a mistake. He called Parliament because he had no choice. Only Parliament could provide the funds for a war to reassert royal authority in Scotland.

SUMMARY QUESTION

1 List the problems facing Charles in 1640. Choose the two you feel are most important and explain why.

CHAPTER 2

The Short and Long Parliaments, 1640–1

THE SHORT PARLIAMENT, APRIL–MAY 1640

Introduction

The Short Parliament proved to be a great disappointment to Charles's hopes. From the beginning distrust of Charles was evident. **MPs were reluctant to support a war against Scottish Protestants** who had rebelled against Laudianism. The comments of MPs were not directed at Charles himself but at Laud and his other advisers and the Roman Catholic circle at Court. While these people had influence over Charles, Parliament was not going to grant the twelve subsidies that Charles requested, even though he linked these to an abandonment of ship money.

The settling of 'grievances'

The Commons, led by John Pym, demanded that 'grievances' should be dealt with before subsidies were voted. At this point Laud characteristically inflamed the situation by issuing a new set of **canons** (instructions to the Church) with clear support for divine right.

The King, rather than haggle with Parliament, dissolved it after only three weeks in **May 1640**. It was to prove a serious mistake as attitudes were to harden after the dissolution. At least in the Short Parliament there had been a significant minority who supported Charles.

The Second Bishops' War, 1640

In July Charles had confiscated bullion (silver coinage) held in the Tower of London for safe keeping by English merchants. After toying with a scheme to use it as a basis for new coins mixed with copper (thus creating a less pure, 'debased' coinage with a smaller amount of gold or silver in it), Charles held on to £30,000-worth as a 'loan'. This, of course, did nothing for his already strained relations with

KEY THEME

MPs' attitude towards Scotland in 1640 The rejection of the new Prayer Book changed many MPs' attitude towards the Scots. Instead of viewing the Scots as cronies at James I's Court looking to England as a land of milk and honey, they now became heroic Protestant resisters.

Laud's canons 1640 Every Church minister was to read aloud the following: 'The most high and sacred order of Kings is of divine nature . . . a supreme power is given to this most excellent order by God himself . . . Kings should rule and command all persons of rank or estate soever . . .'.

Strafford's advice in May 1640 Strafford had urged the calling of a Parliament in 1640 but now took a hard line. He advised Charles 'goe on with a vigorous war, as you first designed, loose and absolved from all rules of government . . . they refusing you are acquitted towards God and man, you have an army in Ireland, you may employ it here to reduce this Kingdome'. This advice was to prove fatal for Strafford later on.

Forty-shilling freeholders Outside of the borough towns, which had differing electoral systems, all those men who owned freehold land worth forty shillings (£2) were entitled to vote in parliamentary elections.

the City of London merchants. These were desperate measures which did nothing to save the situation.

The failure of the Short Parliament was followed by the outbreak of new fighting with the Scots. At a skirmish at Newcastle-upon-Tyne in August 1640 the English were beaten. **Strafford's description of the Scottish advance** in August helps to explain why the Scots were able to capture Newcastle, cutting off London's vital coal supply, and occupy the six northern counties.

> **Strafford's description of the Scottish advance**
> 'the army altogether necessitate [in need] and unprovided . . . that part which I bring now from Durham, the worst ever saw. Our horse [cavalry] all cowardly; the country from Berwick to York in the power of the Scots, a universal affright [fear] in all, a general disaffection to the King's service, non sensible of his dishonour.'

The war was ended by the Treaty of Ripon of October 1640. Negotiated by the Council of Peers it was really a complete humiliation for Charles. The Scots secured £850 per day to cover the costs of occupation of Durham and Northumberland, but also, in effect, as their price for not moving further south. In these circumstances, defeated, and unable to pay the costs of the Scottish occupation, Charles had no choice but to call another Parliament to vote the subsidies required. Personal Rule had finally collapsed and Parliament was called for 3 November 1640.

FROM CRISIS TO CIVIL WAR, 1640–2

The formation of the anti-Court consensus

The elections to the Long Parliament probably saw more people voting than at any time before reform of the electorate in 1832. In some county elections sheriffs did not even check that men were eligible to vote (they had to be **forty-shilling freeholders**) so vast crowds voted and the majority of MPs were well aware of the views of their constituents. 'Choose no Court papist, ship money sheriff' was the cry. Most of those candidates who had been associated with royal policies in the 1630s went down to crushing defeat.

By November 1640 the country gentry going up to Parliament were united in a set of negative attitudes, with a fairly clear idea of what they wanted to stop.

- They were determined to stop the Church becoming more Catholic. They believed that Laudian changes had to be reversed.
- They wanted to punish the King's 'evil counsellors', i.e. Windebank (the Secretary of State) and Finch (a leading royal lawyer) – and especially Laud and Strafford.
- They also wanted to restore the old constitutional balance between the rights of the subject and the rights of the king. They believed that the last ten years had seen an attempt to set up a semi-absolutist state on the continental model.
- They wished to eliminate the financial changes of Personal Rule such as forest fines and ship money.
- They wished to get rid of the hated **Court of Wards**, which had doubled its income during Personal Rule. They also wanted to abolish the **Prerogative Courts: Star Chamber** and **High Commission**.

More generally and most importantly, there was a widespread belief in a Roman Catholic conspiracy centred around members of the Court which was working away to undermine the 'ancient constitution', and, therefore, they wished to 'free' the King from these evil influences.

The fears of the country gentry. Looking at the situation objectively, the King was in a weak position in November 1640, but the country gentry coming up to Parliament were not confident that they had the upper hand. There was a general feeling that this might be the last chance to reverse the trends of the 1630s before England became a Roman Catholic-dominated, absolutist state. They were confident of having the country behind them, but apprehensive about the reactions of Strafford. His record in Ireland and in the Council of the North (the organisation

KEY TERMS

The Courts The **Court of Wards** dealt with under-age heirs to property. The **Prerogative Courts** were controlled by the Crown and were seen as oppressive and unjust: **Star Chamber** punished offenders against various crimes and **High Commission** was the highest Church Court, which dealt with offences involving anything to do with the Church.

that ran the North of England on behalf of the King) indicated a minister who could ruthlessly get things done, and could make absolutism work.

How radical was the anti-Court consensus? So the **anti-Court consensus**, with its fear of a Roman Catholic conspiracy and its hatred of the Court and the King's ministers, was united in what it wanted to prevent and what it wanted to destroy. But the majority had no forward-looking programme of reform, no real idea of creating a new constitution giving more power to Parliament and taking power from the Crown. Therefore they were not revolutionaries seeking to overthrow the King or the constitution.

They had come up to London to restore, not to start a revolution. In that sense they can be seen as conservative. The fact that, with the exception of the 60 or so Court MPs that supported the Crown, they were united on what they disliked does not mean that they shared a vision of what the future should hold. The cement that held them together was negative: fear of popery, fear of absolutism. Nobody in 1640 could know what was to happen by 1642, that a section of Parliament would find itself at war with the King, and nobody could possibly have even contemplated armed rebellion against the King, let alone his eventual execution in 1649.

It is most important that we do not give MPs in 1640 the same motives as they had by 1642 or 1648. Had the conservative country gentry of 1640 realised what was to happen by 1642 and by 1649, they probably would have acted very differently. We know the end of the story, they did not.

THE FIRST SESSION OF THE LONG PARLIAMENT, 1640–1

The first targets of the anti-Court consensus were the King's 'evil counsellors'. Finch and Windebank fled abroad, and Laud was sent to the Tower, finally to be executed in 1645. The main target, however, was Strafford.

The fall of Strafford

Strafford's track record was such that he would be the most marked man in England if the situation ever arose that he could not rely on royal protection.

Thomas Wentworth, Earl of Strafford.

- He, with Laud, had been most associated with the policy of 'thorough', that is ruthlessly carrying out royal wishes and extending royal authority without regard for individuals or, indeed, legal restraints.
- After 1628, when he had supported the Petition of Right (which laid down the rights of Parliament), he went over to the Court. His enemies saw this as apostacy, or changing sides, but from his point of view parliaments had only a limited role and they were there to support the Crown. After the Petition of Right, the King should have expected support from Parliament, not carping or obstruction, so it was logical to further his own career and support royal policies.
- His first important post was President of the Council of the North, where he had become notorious for riding roughshod over local rights and treating the gentry with arrogance. Despite the ideal of 'thorough' being one of honest administration, he had managed to do very well for himself, although no more so than any other seventeenth-century statesman.
- In 1633 he went to **Ireland** as Lord Deputy. Strafford reduced Ireland to obedience, something never before achieved, but it was at the cost of being hated in Ireland and feared in England. The English gentry took the view that what he had achieved in Ireland he could do in England. The Irish Parliament was reduced to a 'rubber stamp', just voting taxes to support Strafford's new Irish army. The Irish Church was remodelled on Laudian lines, much to the resentment of the Scottish Presbyterian settlers of Ulster. Strafford also made sure that powerful individuals knew their place, the most notable of whom was the Earl of Cork. He alleged that Strafford had taken £40,000 of his personal estate and ridden roughshod over the law to do it. At Strafford's trial, Cork testified to the Lord Deputy's dictatorial methods saying that he had declared: 'I tell you, I will not have my orders disputed by law or lawyers.'

KEY THEME

Ireland had always been a thorn in the side of royal administrators. In some ways the great Anglo-Irish lords and landowners and the Scottish Presbyterian settlers were independent of London and used to being able to do as they wished. The Roman Catholic Irish, gradually being pushed out of their lands by the Scots and English, resented English government from a different point of view.

The Commons were determined to eliminate the threat of such a ruthless and dynamic minister. As soon as Parliament met, Strafford was impeached (brought to trial before Parliament). This was mainly on the charge of wishing to bring his Irish army over to use as a force to continue Personal Rule by setting up a royal military dictatorship. The advice that he had given to Charles after the dissolution of the Short Parliament now rebounded on him.

Strafford's trial, May 1641. In fact, evidence of actual treachery was difficult to obtain. **Pym**, as leader of the Commons, had to resort to an **Act of Attainder**. This needed less precise evidence but was legally dubious. The London mob was putting pressure on the Lords to pass the Act and it seems the Lords, who although they had no love for Strafford were becoming worried about the implications of such a vague legal charge, passed the Act under the impression that Charles would never sign it. He had already promised Strafford that he would not suffer in 'either life or fortune' but, as so often when under pressure, Charles wavered and Strafford was executed on 12 May. It appears that Charles was really worried about a popular

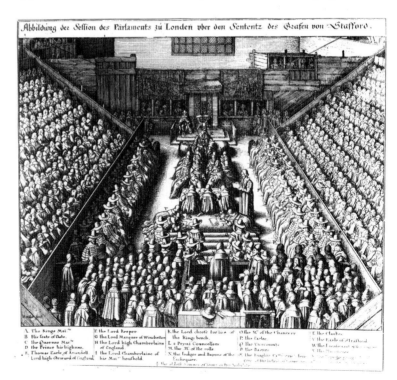

Abbildung der Session des Parlaments zu Londen vber den Sententz des Grafen von Stafford.

The trial of Strafford.

uprising if he did not pass the Act, but Laud's comment is pointed: 'he [Strafford] served a mild and gracious prince who knew not how to be, or could be made great'.

John Pym.

John Pym 1583–1643

MP for Tavistock, by 1628 Pym was a leading opponent of Charles I's policies and the rise of Laudianism. He dominated the Short Parliament of May 1640 and the Long Parliament until his death.

Convinced of the existence of a Roman Catholic conspiracy, Pym was able, for much of the time, to carry the majority of the House of Commons with him. His control over the House led to his being called 'King Pym'. He was responsible for drawing up all the measures that the Long Parliament passed in 1641 as well as the Nineteen Propositions of 1642 that led to civil war. No other figure, save Charles himself, was so important in the period.

The destruction of the machinery of Personal Rule, spring 1641

At the same time the Commons, with Pym as leader, assaulted all the machinery of Personal Rule. The Courts of Star Chamber and High Commission were abolished, depriving the King and the Church of their most powerful legal weapons.

- Ship money was declared illegal.
- Boundaries of royal forests were declared to be those of the twentieth year of James's reign.
- Distraint of knighthood (fining people for refusing a knighthood) was also declared to be illegal.
- The Court of Wards was abolished.

All these acts to which Charles agreed, however reluctantly, can be seen as re-establishing the 'old constitution', but the **Triennial Act**, signed by Charles on the same day that he signed Strafford's attainder, cannot. The Triennial Act was revolutionary, and why Charles agreed to it is, on the face of it, puzzling. It is possible that, as he was agonising over

KEY TERM

The **Triennal Act** laid down that a Parliament must be called no later than three years after the dissolution of its predecessor. This took away the royal prerogative of calling parliaments only when the monarch needed them.

Strafford's fate, and the London mob, probably encouraged by Pym's supporters in the City, was active, he failed fully to realise the significance of what he was agreeing to. On the other hand, given his capacity to be devious, Charles may well have seen this as a temporary concession which, when he was in a stronger position, he would be able to withdraw again.

The anti-Court consensus holds firm. Until the summer of 1641 the anti-Court consensus held reasonably intact, although some members already had misgivings about the legality of Strafford's execution and about an **act for 'a perpetual parliament'** (a Parliament without end). That the consensus held is partly due to Pym's skill. He and his associates, such as Vane and St John, were able to present these measures as necessary to safeguard the freedoms of the House of Commons and as restoring the balance of the constitution. Pym was particularly good at playing on fears of popery, and he fully supported the idea that there was a Roman Catholic conspiracy that still needed to be fully dealt with. A vague 'army plot' in the spring of 1641, involving officers around the Court possibly planning some coup, only helped Pym's thesis.

The events of 1641–2 can only be fully understood if one realises the great fear of such a conspiracy, and the atmosphere of crisis in which the Long Parliament, for some of the time, was meeting.

The death of Bedford. A significant event in May 1641 was the death of **Francis Russell, Earl of Bedford**. A bridge between Parliament and the King could possibly have been constructed by Bedford. St John had become Solicitor General in January 1641. He was a close associate of Pym and had defended Hampden in the Ship Money Case of 1637 (when Hampden had opposed the King's right to collect the tax). Several opposition peers, including Bedford and Essex, had been appointed to the Privy Council. By May it seemed that Bedford was arranging for Pym to be Chancellor of the Exchequer, while the Secretary of State was to be Denzil Holles, at that time a Pym associate.

Act for 'a perpetual parliament' By an act passed in May 1641 Parliament could not be dissolved by the King but only by its own consent.

KEY PERSON

Francis Russell, Earl of Bedford Bedford was a man with a foot in both camps. He was a courtier but had good relations with some of the leading Parliament men. Pym sat for a seat over which Bedford had control and Pym also looked after some of the Russell family affairs. Bedford was a moderate and probably hoped to organise a government that would have the confidence of the House of Commons, Lords and the King.

Francis Russell, Earl of Bedford.

If anyone could have built a 'government of national confidence' it was Bedford. He had access to and was listened to by Charles. His death, then, removed a very important chance of compromise.

The Ten Propositions, June 1641. By the summer, Pym had set out his position in the Ten Propositions. These included a request to the King to commit 'his own business and the affairs of the Kingdom to such councillors and officers as the Parliament may have cause to confide in'. Like the Triennial Act, this demand, that Parliament should in effect choose the King's ministers, took away some of the King's powers, but Pym never, from that moment on, wavered in this aim. Given that the demand was revolutionary why did a conservative House of Commons accept it?

- Firstly, Pym presented these demands as being 'defensive'; ensuring that all the laws passed already would be protected by having some control over ministers who had access to the King.
- Secondly, until the Grand Remonstrance of November 1641 (see page 25), or indeed the Nineteen Propositions of June 1642 (see page 31), many members may not have understood Pym's position.
- Thirdly, given that the Bedford scheme, of which many had high hopes, had seemed to collapse, not because of Charles's opposition but because of Bedford's death, it may have seemed a reasonable demand which the King would have been inclined to accept.

The problem was sidelined by the King's decision to go north and visit Scotland, and a six-week recess of Parliament.

POTENTIAL FURTHER PROBLEMS

Despite the general agreement of most of the MPs in the first session, under the surface there were cracks that Pym was plastering over:

- the question of the future organisation of the Church was one,
- another was the role of Parliament in relation to the royal prerogative, which many MPs saw as part of a balanced constitution.

The 'Root and Branch' Petition. One potentially divisive issue had already been raised in February 1641. The London 'Root and Branch' Petition called for the abolition of bishops. Many MPs had no love for high-handed Laudian bishops but that did not mean that they wished to see episcopacy (rule of the Church by bishops) abolished altogether. They wanted the moderate bishops of Elizabeth's time, not a Presbyterian system (rule of the Church by elders). Pym, whatever his private views, realised this issue was potentially one which would divide the Commons, so he deflected it in the usual style of a politician who has an awkward problem – it was given to a committee to discuss, the Assembly of Divines.

CONCLUSION

The first session of the Long Parliament, then, had been one which the majority of the country MPs were satisfied with. There was still a lurking fear of a Roman Catholic conspiracy, and some MPs were beginning to have doubts about Pym's use of the mob to pressurise the Lords into passing measures, but his skill at keeping the Commons together meant that, until the summer of 1641, the Commons were reasonably united.

More broadly, the aims of the anti-Court consensus had been largely achieved by the summer of 1641, so where did Parliament go next? Was there any need for further legislation? Could Charles now be trusted to rule in a 'mixed constitution' and not return to his absolutist leanings if Parliament dissolved itself? These were unspoken questions in the summer of 1641 but they were there in the minds of many MPs. Pym's achievement had been to keep the largely negative anti-Court consensus together, but this was going to become increasingly difficult. However, distrust of Charles was still a strong factor holding Parliament together.

SUMMARY QUESTIONS

1 Why did the Short Parliament fail?

2 Sum up the attitudes of MPs towards Charles in 1640.

3 Draw up a timeline of what you see as the ten most significant events of 1641. Explain the significance of each event you have chosen.

CHAPTER 3

Crisis, confrontation and civil war, 1641–2

CRISIS AND CONFRONTATION, 1641–2

Charles in Scotland

When Charles left for Scotland to ratify the treaty between the two countries, there was a fear that he hoped to woo the Scots into providing him with an army. Parliament actually sent commissioners with Charles to watch him. In fact, events in Scotland only fuelled fears about Charles's trustworthiness. Although some Scots were by now disillusioned with the Covenanters, 'the incident', in which extremist Scottish royalists tried to capture the Covenanter leaders, destroyed any hope of Charles coming to an agreement with his Scottish subjects. He may not have known of 'the incident' but in England parallels were drawn with the army plot of spring 1641, and Charles's integrity was again damaged.

The second session of Parliament

When Parliament reassembled in October 1641, the potential splits began to be apparent. Pym was convinced that Charles was not to be trusted; that, if Parliament did not put further restraints on royal power, once Parliament dissolved itself Charles would go back to his absolutist tendencies.

The role of Henrietta Maria. Having eliminated the previous 'evil counsellors', Pym now saw **Henrietta Maria** and her associates at Court as being the most dangerous influence over Charles. Henrietta Maria never understood the concepts behind the English constitution. Parliaments were hateful to her: kings ruled, subjects obeyed.

Support for Charles appears. At the same time, a group emerged in the House of Commons who could be called the 'Constitutional Royalists'. Their leading members were

KEY THEME

The role of Henrietta Maria She certainly encouraged Charles to resist parliamentary demands and, more dangerously, encouraged some of the more hot-headed members of her circle into contemplating military coups to remove the 'rebellious' leaders of the Commons.

Hyde, Falkland and Culpepper. These were true 'conservatives'; they had opposed the royal policies of the 1630s as being radical and undermining the constitution. They had disliked Laudian changes to the Church and had agreed to the execution of Strafford. Now their conservatism made them concerned for the future. The reforms of 1641 had restored the balance between the King and Parliament, and the Anglican Church was now back to its proper position with the fall of the Laudian bishops. Their concern now was that extremist Puritans would actually destroy the Church of England and that Pym's policies would lead to constitutional change or, worse, anarchy. They believed that now the King *must* be trusted or the constitution could not work.

Edward Hyde (later Earl of Clarendon) 1609–74

MP for Saltash in Cornwall in the Long Parliament, Hyde was a conservative moderate but attacked Strafford and all the machinery of Personal Rule. He then became alarmed at the direction in which Pym and his associates were going. Strongly Anglican, he objected to moves to exclude the bishops from the House of Lords. Trying to persuade the King to rule according to the constitution, he sensed that the 'conservative side' of many MPs would be won away from Pym if the King was to set himself up as the defender of the constitution. Hyde was not consulted about the Five Members Coup (see pages 28–9) and was horrified by it. He had already drawn up the King's moderate reply to the Grand Remonstrance and was effective in the 'paper war' of 1642, again drawing up the King's reply to the Nineteen Propositions (see page 31). An opponent of the extreme attitudes of Henrietta Maria and Digby, Hyde went abroad with the Prince of Wales in 1646. He wrote his *History of the Great Rebellion* in exile and was created Earl of Clarendon at the Restoration of Charles II.

Edward Hyde.

Had Charles consistently taken the advice of the Constitutional Royalists, it is quite possible that he would have avoided disaster. Many MPs were sympathetic to the views of the Constitutional Royalists and there were signs

KEY THEME

The Grand Remonstrance
Most of the Remonstrance went over past history, reminding MPs of Charles's policies in the 1630s. It emphasised the so-called 'evidence' of a Roman Catholic conspiracy: 'the root of all this mischief we find to be a malignant design [plan] of subverting [undermining] the fundamental laws and principles of Government, upon which the religion and justice of this Kingdom are firmly established'.

The Remonstrance ended with demands that the laws against Roman Catholics should be strictly enforced, that the House of Commons should be able to remove the King's ministers, and that he should 'employ such councillors, ambassadors, and other ministers in managing his business at home and abroad, as [Parliament had confidence] in'.

that in the autumn of 1641 Charles was becoming more popular. This may be partly in reaction to:

- the increasing activities of religious radicals, accompanied by a growth in unauthorised preaching and disturbances in churches;
- increasing unrest among the 'lower orders', partly caused by a trade depression.

In these circumstances the King represented stability.

So, if Charles had consistently followed the moderate constitutional path advised by Hyde and Falkland, he could have presented himself as the symbol of order and stability. He might also have seemed to be a trustworthy monarch who would rule according to the law, respecting his subjects' rights while protecting his own rights. This might have undermined Pym's position, because Pym's use of the **mob** and his apparent desire to push on with further constitutional changes were beginning to cause alarm in the House of Commons among a naturally conservative gentry.

The Grand Remonstrance. Pym was determined to press on. He genuinely believed in a Roman Catholic underground conspiracy manipulating the King, but he also feared for his own life if the King could regain total freedom of action. He was aware of the sort of advice Charles was getting from Henrietta Maria and that he was tempted to follow it. The gradual erosion of the anti-Court consensus, combined with Pym's fears of Charles's motives and the Roman Catholic circle at Court, led Pym to draw up the **Grand Remonstrance**. This was not the self-confident sign of a strong position that it seemed, but a desperate measure.

The break-up of the anti-Court consensus. The Grand Remonstrance was drawn up during October and presented to the Commons in November 1641. Much of the Remonstrance can be seen as propaganda, designed to remind members of the past actions of Charles, to reassert the existence of a Roman Catholic conspiracy, and to justify at the end what was clearly a 'revolutionary' series of demands. These included the right of the Commons to choose the King's ministers (harking back to the Ten

Propositions of June) and the right to reform the Church. These were clear invasions of the royal prerogative and could not be seen as restoring the 'old constitution'.

- The Grand Remonstrance caused the break up of the anti-Court consensus. It was passed after heated debates, including drawn swords in the House, by 159 to 148. There was now the making of a 'King's Party' in the House, prepared to defend the old constitution.
- What had disturbed many members were Pym's methods to put pressure for a favourable vote – again using the mob.
- The Remonstrance was printed and published and this, for many conservatives, was the last straw. Sir Edward Dering, a Kentish MP, who had supported all the innovations of the past year, spoke for many when he said: 'I did not dream that we should remonstrate downwards, tell tales to the people and speak of the King as of a third person.' The conservative gentry, already disturbed by Pym's willingness to use the 'lower orders' to bring political pressure on the House of Lords, were horrified that 'the people' were being involved in politics by Pym's printing of the Remonstrance.
- Some MPs were already very disturbed at the signs of public disorder, with unauthorised preaching, floods of **pamphlets** and rioting. Anarchy could now be seen as a threat as great as Charles's absolutist policies.

The King's reply to the Remonstrance. The King's reply to the Remonstrance was moderate. It was designed to reassure members that, while he was prepared to defend his legal rights, he was also defending the rights of his subjects.

The Irish Rebellion – the crisis deepens

However, another event had increased the tempo of the crisis. On 1 November the news of the Irish Rebellion broke. The Catholic native Irish, now that the oppressive rule of Strafford had been removed, rose in rebellion against the Ulster Presbyterians. Probably 4000 Protestants died in massacres and perhaps another 8000 from exposure as they fled their homes or were thrust out in winter. Horror stories, which lost nothing in the telling, spread quickly and absurd estimates of the numbers killed circulated.

Pamphlets Press censorship disappeared with the Long Parliament so many people produced pamphlets suggesting religious or political changes. They would be printed and distributed to as many people as possible.

The Irish Rebellion.

- Damagingly for Charles, the rebels claimed, falsely, to be acting in his name.
- As the full implication of the revolt sank in, one question was paramount. An army would have to be raised to put down the rebellion. As far as the traditional constitution was concerned, the King had the undoubted right to command the army.
- The question, therefore, was: could Charles be trusted with an army? Would he use it to put down the revolt in Ulster or his opponents at Westminster?
- The Irish Rebellion also strengthened the belief in a Roman Catholic conspiracy.

Charles's mistakes during the Irish Crisis – the turning point. This was the turning point of the period 1640–2. If Charles had consistently given the impression that he was now prepared to rule according to the constitution and was not still hoping to regain the position that he had in the 1630s, the crisis could have been defused. Unfortunately, Charles never pursued one consistent policy. At this point, feeling more self-confident, he listened to the 'absolutist' clique at Court led by Henrietta Maria. Thomas Lunsford, a soldier of fortune, popularly supposed to be the sort of adventurer who would involve himself in a military coup, was appointed governor of the Tower of London by Charles. This was a key appointment, with its capacity to overawe the City. It seemed to be a confirmation of Charles's secret desire to regain freedom of action through a military coup but, under pressure, Charles then cancelled the appointment. He sent two equally damaging signals:

- firstly, that he had thought about a coup;
- secondly, that he was weak and could be forced to back down.

Charles made a further mistake in failing to appoint a commander for the troops to be raised for the reconquest of Ireland. Had Charles appointed the Earl of Essex, that would have been a military appointment which would have reassured the House of Commons, as Essex was associated with all the reforms of the past year, but Charles failed to do so.

The Five Members Coup, January 1642

Still listening to **George Digby** and **Henrietta Maria**, Charles then made a fatal error. Believing that an impeachment of the Queen was being contemplated by Pym and his supporters, he impeached Lord Mandeville and the MPs Pym, Hampden, Strode, Heselrige and Holles – the so-called Five Members. The impeachment sent to the Lords was not acted on, and Charles decided to take matters into his own hands. On 5 January 1642 he entered the House of Commons with 300 troops to arrest the Five Members. They had prior knowledge of his intentions and were safely in the City.

- The Commons were outraged by this breach of privilege, the King was surrounded by an angry mob as he left the Commons and the Five Members returned in triumph.

KEY PERSON

George Digby (Second Earl of Bristol) 1612–77 By 1641 he was a principal adviser to Henrietta Maria. Digby consistently undermined attempts by the Constitutional Royalists to persuade Charles into a moderate line. He became a Roman Catholic. Digby was a leading figure in the decision to attempt the Five Members Coup, and continued as a damaging absolutist influence over Charles during the Civil War. He also intrigued against Prince Rupert and other successful Royalist commanders. He later fled to France. His advice to Charles was usually disastrous, both before and during the Civil War.

KEY THEME

Henrietta Maria's advice
to Charles was consistently of 'no compromise'. A letter of hers to Charles in March 1642 gives a flavour of her views: 'a report is current here that you are returning to London . . . I believe nothing of it and hope you are more constant in your resolutions, you have already learnt, to your cost, that want of perseverance . . . has ruined you. But if it be so adieu: for assuredly you will never change my resolution to retire into a convent, for I can never trust myself to those persons who would be your directors, nor to you sire, you would have broken your promise to me.'

- Given the temper of the population, Charles seems to have literally feared for his life for, on 10 January, he left London.

The effect of the Five Members Coup.
- The whole affair of the Five Members made civil war more likely.
- It swung many Members of Parliament back to Pym, as this was the military coup that he had been predicting: a coup encouraged by Roman Catholics.
- The King leaving London was also crucial: two sides now had to negotiate at a distance.

It is difficult to judge what Charles was preparing to do once he had left London. At first, he attempted to gain control of arsenals at Portsmouth, Kingston-upon-Thames and, most importantly, Hull, but failed. The Queen left for France to seek support for her husband. Charles then appears to have listened to the advice of Hyde again. Hyde started to produce moderate Royalist propaganda that was quite convincing. This pointed out that the King had constitutional rights which Parliament and Pym seemed to be attacking. The inconsistent pattern of Charles's behaviour, however, became apparent once more: Charles wavered between concession and compromise on the one hand, and active preparations for war on the other.

Charles's entry into Parliament.

THE DRIFT TO CIVIL WAR, JANUARY–AUGUST 1642

The impossibility of compromise

'We sink unsensibly into this state of civil war' was the comment of Sir Harbottle Grimston, and in some ways he was right. The period January to August 1642 saw developments which made any compromise impossible.

- **Social and religious unrest.** There was widespread social disorder, with rioting in the Stour valley among the weavers, and in the Fens. A poor harvest and a trade depression – 'the trade of this Kingdom stoppeth altogether', noted the Venetian ambassador with some exaggeration – meant that there was considerable distress among the 'lower orders'. The gentry found these signs of potential unrest most disturbing to the social order, and the growth of radical preaching and pamphleteering also seemed to threaten stability.
- **The collapse of authority.** In practice, there had developed two rival authorities – the King in the North and Parliament in London. A potential power vacuum was therefore being created, and the collapse of the authority of the Church of England only served to make the future seem bleaker for those who saw the cement that held society together beginning to crumble. In these circumstances some of the gentry were arming themselves, fearing the country would slide into anarchy.
- **Propaganda.** A war of words was conducted between the King and Parliament throughout the spring and summer, each hoping to persuade the uncommitted or moderates of the justice of their cause, and to convince the other side of their strength.

The Militia Ordinance and Commission of Array

In March 1642 Parliament took another step on the road to war by issuing the Militia Ordinance, appointing officers to the militia and ordering them to make sure the militia was prepared. In theory, only the King could do this, but he naturally refused parliamentary requests that they should be able to appoint the deputy lieutenants and officers. In these circumstances Parliament acted alone to put the country into 'a posture of defence by authority of both houses'. The King replied with the Commission of

Array – a 'call up' of even more dubious legality. Each side, then, was trying to secure the county militias to frighten the other side into surrender. In fact, the Commission of Array, a very ancient legal device, was not accepted by many; a judge in the West Country noted in a letter to the King, 'the truth is the counties are much possessed with the illegality of the Commissions of Array and the unlimited power as is alleged in the Commissions'.

- The King did not have a great deal of success in getting the county militias to support him, and Parliament's position, by the summer, seemed to be stronger militarily despite Hyde's skilful Royalist propaganda.
- The majority of the gentry either supported the Militia Ordinance 'for the defence of the King and Parliament', or seemed to be trying to stay neutral.

The Nineteen Propositions, June 1642

Pym then felt confident enough to present the **Nineteen Propositions** to the King. They were so uncompromising that they could not be said to be a negotiating position at all. These demands would have made Charles almost a constitutional monarch in the modern sense of the word. As it was, Charles was left with no choice. Acceptance of the propositions, which were revolutionary in seventeenth-century terms, would have been unthinkable, especially to a monarch who believed in his divine right to rule.

Charles declares war

Charles chose instead to raise his standard at Nottingham on 22 August 1642 and formally declare war on Parliament.

- Pym probably thought, as others did, that this was an empty, futile gesture – the King had only 800 supporters with him and, therefore, if there was to be any fighting, it would only be a skirmish or two before Charles saw the logic of his position and accepted the Nineteen Propositions.
- The Parliamentary leaders had badly miscalculated; the First Civil War was to last for four years and cost the lives of at least 50,000 Englishmen.
- Many of these Englishmen would have been mystified as to how England had drifted into 'this state of civil war',

a war that probably nobody, except a few hotheads mostly on the King's side, wanted.

- Even at this stage, it is possible that the crisis could have been settled 'with some showers of blood', rather than 'effusions of blood', as one Norfolk gentleman hoped. However, Parliament's next move, again probably the result of over-confidence, ensured that at last the King got a sizeable army. On 6 September a Parliamentary declaration stated that those who did not actively support Parliament were to be declared 'delinquents' and made to pay for the cost of the war.
- This finally drove those members of the gentry who favoured the King but who wished to remain neutral into making up their minds. Neutrality was no longer an option for them. Within weeks the King had a sizeable army and a long war was afoot.

CONCLUSION – WHY CIVIL WAR BROKE OUT IN 1642

Key ideas

None of the gentry coming up to Parliament in 1640 were thinking in terms of war. They were 'conservatives' hoping to restore a balance that the King's policies of the 1630s had destroyed. In theory, therefore, there is nothing inevitable about the crisis of 1640 leading to civil war. The following were the important factors and events that transformed the situation.

- **Charles's inability to pursue a consistent policy.** He must take a fair share of the blame for the events of 1641–2. He granted concessions reluctantly, thus giving the impression either that he could always, in the last resort, be pushed into capitulation or that, if he had freedom of action, Personal Rule would return.
- **The actions of Pym and his associates.** They were determined to put further restraints on the King. Pym may have had ambitions to be 'first minister' or it may be that he, and his close associates, were genuinely scared of a royal comeback which would be followed by their execution. Of course, Pym may have been a 'reformer' believing the old constitution could no longer work; the

Nineteen Propositions can be seen as evidence of this. On the other hand, they can be seen as a reaction to the untrustworthiness of Charles, rather than a planned, permanent constitutional reform.

- **The Irish Rebellion** is, perhaps, the single most important factor that transformed the situation in the autumn of 1641. It created a crisis because the question of command of the armed forces was no longer a theoretical one but a pressing practical one. Neither Pym nor the King could give way on this. It also strengthened the fear of a Roman Catholic conspiracy (see page 79), and MPs were no longer 'thinking things through calmly'.
- **The Five Members Coup** outraged both the Lords and the Commons, restored Pym's position and confirmed Charles as dangerously untrustworthy. Charles's subsequent panic move from London made civil war a real possibility, as he then tried to take over arsenals of weapons in various parts of the country.
- **The Militia Ordinance and Commissions of Array** started the dangerous process of choosing sides and raising troops, making war more possible.
- **The Nineteen Propositions** were the last straw for Charles, who formally went to war to save his prerogative, but they also showed the deep divide between the King's and Parliament's views of how the constitution should operate, and what it should be. The divide could not be bridged by negotiation.
- **The Parliamentary declaration of 6 September** transformed Charles's military position from weakness to strength, making an actual serious 'shooting war' possible because the King was able to raise an army.

SUMMARY QUESTIONS

1 Why was the Irish Crisis so important as a turning point on the road to civil war?

2 What do you feel are the three most important long-term reasons for the outbreak of the First Civil War and the three most important short-term reasons? Explain your choices fully.

CHAPTER 4

The military history of the First Civil War, 1642–6

THE TWO SIDES

The King

In one respect, once he raised an army, the King had advantages over Parliament in the early months of the war. His cavalry were probably better and he had a cavalry commander of talent in his German nephew Prince Rupert.

Parliament

In other respects, especially if the war dragged on, Parliament held most of the cards. The navy, unpaid by Charles, mostly went over to Parliament, probably due to the popularity of the Earl of Warwick who had been appointed its commander by Parliament.

Importance of the navy. Command of the sea was vital for two reasons:

- Firstly, with a large percentage of internal as well as external trade going by sea, and with a Parliamentary navy in control, London could continue to be England's trading capital.
- Secondly, Charles could be prevented from importing much-needed arms from abroad, nor could he hope for troops from any of his neighbouring monarchs to assist him.

Parliament's financial advantage. Parliament controlled the more populated and prosperous part of the kingdom, as well as that vital source of wealth – London. The King's area of control was the poorer north and west.

- Once Pym had set up efficient tax-gathering mechanisms, such as the monthly assessment, and a

Charles I and Sir
Edward Walker, his
military secretary.

well-organised system of exploiting the estates of
Royalist supporters living in Parliamentary areas –
compounding – then Parliament's war finances were on
a sounder footing than those of Charles.

- Charles had to rely partly on individual gifts, plus the
gold and silver plate given by Oxford colleges, and the
fact that many of his commanders paid their troops out
of their own pocket. Royalist fund-raising was well
organised in some areas but, as a broad generalisation,
lack of pay made Royalist troops more inclined to ill-
discipline and plunder.
- As time went on the King's shortage of money became
one of the major factors in his eventual defeat – 'the
incurable disease of want of money' as Clarendon
described it.
- Therefore, it can be argued that, apart from his
opponents making a fatal military error, the only war
that Charles could win was a short one although this was
by no means clear at the time.

THE OPENING MOVES

At the beginning of the war, and indeed before formal
hostilities started, both sides tried to seize county and local
arsenals to equip their supporters. The failure, on two
occasions, to gain control of the great northern arsenal at

Hull was a very significant setback for the King. The militias proved lukewarm and militarily useless in general, so the militia were often gathered together and disarmed, their weapons being given to those who were prepared to fight. The only exceptions to the general ineffectiveness of the militias were the Cornish Trained Bands who fought for the King and the London Trained Bands who saved the Parliamentary cause on two occasions.

Charles's advance on London

The autumn of 1642 saw Charles advancing slowly on London with an army of about 10,000. The Parliamentary commander, the **Earl of Essex**, had been chosen on two grounds: firstly, he did have some military experience and, secondly, as a peer, he gave status to the Parliamentary cause. But he was a cautious and indeed rather uninspiring

The Earl of Essex.

leader. He even carried his coffin with him on his military campaigns, which was not calculated to raise morale.

The Battle of Edgehill, October 1642

The two armies met at Edgehill. The Royalist superiority in cavalry made itself felt as they swept the Parliamentary cavalry away, but the Parliamentary infantry proceeded to defeat their Royalist counterparts and the Royalists were only saved by the reappearance of their cavalry. Essex withdrew, leaving the way open to London, so if the battle can be seen as a draw it was certainly a draw that was to the King's advantage.

The King's moves after Edgehill

At this stage, a swift advance on London might have resulted in a Royalist victory but the King, perhaps shaken by the first battle he had witnessed, moved too hesitantly, taking time out to capture Oxford before advancing on London.

In November 1642 Essex and his army made their way to London in front of the King. The Londoners turned out in their thousands, women helped to dig trenches and, by the time Prince Rupert was burning Brentford (he usually burnt everyplace he captured as he had learnt his trade in the brutal warfare of the Thirty Years War), Essex may have had 24,000 under his command ready to defend the City at Turnham Green, on the outskirts of London.

- It is possible that, if Charles had listened to Rupert's urgings to force the defences at Turnham Green, then the raw citizen soldiers of London would have panicked and fled. It is equally possible that the Royalists would have been overwhelmed in bitter hand-to-hand street fighting by the inhabitants of London, eager to defend their property against Royalists, already notorious for plundering.
- What can be argued is that Charles's failure to fight at Turnham Green, and his withdrawal to Oxford, not only ensured that the First Civil War would go on, but that he threw away his best chance of a quick victory and therefore, in the long run, lost the whole war.

Prince Rupert 1619–82 (Rupert of the Rhine)

A son of the Elector Palatine Frederick and the daughter of James I, Rupert was therefore a nephew of Charles I. He fought in the Thirty Years War but spent some time as a prisoner. He was an inspiring leader of cavalry, very skilled in the cavalry skirmishes that were such a feature of the Civil War. He became the hero of the Royalists for his swift actions, bravery and general youthful dash.

- As a commander of large forces in pitched battles he was not so competent. He failed to see the 'big picture' as at Naseby when his cavalry did break the opposing Parliamentary cavalry on his wing but then charged off the battlefield to attack (and loot) baggage waggons. Cromwell always controlled his cavalry, making them halt after actions to regroup and attack again.
- Rupert also gained a reputation for ruthlessness with the slaughter of defenders at Bolton in 1644 and Leicester in 1645. He was probably correct to surrender Bristol in September 1645 but, at the promptings of Digby, who always seems to have schemed against him, Charles dismissed him from command. Later in 1649 he became a 'privateer' commanding a small fleet that preyed on Parliamentary shipping.
- His reputation is probably rather overrated. He was certainly a better commander than Newcastle, who commanded in the north, or George Goring – hardly stiff competition – but Sir Ralph Hopton, the Royalist commander in the west, was probably a better soldier. It is his dashing character and youth that have given Rupert his reputation.

Prince Rupert.

THE ARMIES OF 1643

By the spring of 1643 most attempts to remain neutral had broken down and several armies were in the field. For the King, the Duke of Newcastle commanded the Northern

Royalist held territory

Parliamentary territory

Disputed territory

England, winter 1642, showing how the country was divided.

army, Sir Ralph Hopton his army in the west, with the support of the cavalry of the not very sober Sir George Goring. The King's main field army was centred around Oxford, with Rupert commanding the cavalry.

For Parliament, Essex remained in charge of their main field army, with the Eastern Association (Norfolk, Suffolk, Cambridge, Huntingdon and Lincolnshire) providing an army under the **Earl of Manchester**. Manchester was another hesitant commander. The Parliamentary Western army was under the command of Sir William Waller, while in Yorkshire the Fairfaxes, father and son, fought against Newcastle from the clothing-town strongholds of Leeds and Bradford. Despite the dash and skill of the younger Fairfax, Sir Thomas, it was a battle against the odds.

Charles's strategy in 1643

In 1643 Charles may have planned a three-pronged attack on the areas held by Parliament, designed to force his way to London which he intended to besiege into surrender. Whether or not planned there were the following moves:

- Newcastle moving south through Yorkshire and Lincolnshire;

- the King's main field army moving up the Thames Valley from Oxford towards London;
- Sir Ralph Hopton's forces advancing through the southern counties heading for Kent.

This sensible plan presented the most serious threat to Parliament and made 1643 a crisis year for Pym. However, the strategy broke down during the course of the year.

Newcastle's failure. Newcastle advanced into Lincolnshire, threatening the Eastern Association heartland. Then, nearing Stamford in the extreme south of Lincolnshire, he decided to retreat and besiege Hull with his main forces. This decision seems to have been the result of some sharp checks his forces had received from **Oliver Cromwell**'s newly trained cavalry. His supply lines had also become

The Earl of Manchester 1602–71 Parliament was anxious to have aristocrats in command in 1642 to give respectability to the cause. As Viscount Mandeville he had been 'marked down', charged with treason, by Charles at the time of the Five Members Coup. He commanded the Eastern Association army and was to fall out with Oliver Cromwell over his hesitant attitude to fighting to the finish, throwing away advantages that he had after Marston Moor and the second Battle of Newbury in 1644. He was a Presbyterian who encouraged the wholesale smashing of stained glass windows and statues in churches.

Manchester, together with the Earl of Essex, was removed from command by the Self-Denying Ordinance of 1645. This said that no peer or MP could hold military office.

The Earl of Manchester.

stretched and he was fearful of an attack on his rear by the Hull garrison. The war in the East then returned to being a series of cavalry raids and skirmishes rather than a determined and dangerous Royalist advance.

Hopton's failure. Sir Ralph Hopton's attack in the South through Hampshire and into Sussex was the most successful but again extended supply lines eventually halted him. His troops were also reluctant to march too far from their home counties – a problem faced by all commanders on all sides.

The siege of Gloucester and Battle of Newbury. As his strategy had broken down Charles decided to besiege Gloucester, which held out for Parliament in the Royalist West and had an important position across Charles's supply lines. The fall of Gloucester would have had a catastrophic effect on already shaken Parliamentary morale for, although the King's strategy was already breaking down, Parliament had not had any decisive victories and the initiative seemed still to be with the King. Essex relieved Gloucester and, on his return march to London, found the King barring his path at Newbury on 20 September 1643. The first Battle of Newbury was a draw but a strategic victory for Essex in that his forces were able to continue their march to London.

'OUTSIDE' HELP

In the autumn of 1643 both sides, after a year of indecisive fighting, tried to swing the balance in their direction by calling upon outside help. The King negotiated a ceasefire or cessation of arms (known as the **Cessation**) with the Irish rebels to allow him to bring English regiments back from Ireland. Parliament negotiated help from the Scots. The Solemn League and Covenant (see page 51) between Parliament and the Scots was signed in September 1643. It meant that Scottish forces coming south would trap Newcastle's army between them and the Eastern Association. The Scottish contribution was a significant one and was Pym's last act towards Parliamentary victory; he died on 8 December 1643.

Major battles of the First Civil War.

The role of the Scots

The Scots, under the Earl of Leven, crossed the border in January 1644. Newcastle's immediate problem was to prevent the Scots joining up with Fairfax's Hull troops. The temporary commander of the Yorkshire Royalists, Lord Bellasis, threw away the Royalist position in the north. Bellasis was defeated by Fairfax at Selby in April 1644, and Newcastle, who had moved north to face the Scots, now had an unprotected rear. The Eastern Association army was moving north to support Fairfax, and Newcastle retreated into York caught in the vice. Prince Rupert rushed to his relief and actually managed to raise the Parliamentary siege of York.

The Battle of Marston Moor, July 1644. Rupert then made an error. He offered battle at Marston Moor on 2 July 1644. The more sensible move would have been to gather all of Newcastle's and his own forces and retreat (as Newcastle advised) – his was, after all, the inferior force, perhaps 9000 fewer than the Parliamentarians. Rupert may have believed that his orders from the King were that he should offer battle but in any case his dynamic, ruthless attitude to war made him want to offer battle if he possibly could. But the real misjudgement was that, as it was drawing on towards evening, he assumed there would be no battle that day. The Parliamentarians, with Cromwell's cavalry in the lead, attacked and the King's Northern army was destroyed. Significantly, the Eastern Association cavalry showed themselves to be a match for the Royalist horse. Newcastle's own regiment, the Whitecoats, died to a man – not **Newcastle**, he left for the continent. Rupert managed to cut himself free with about 6000 men but the King had lost the north. York surrendered within a fortnight.

Marston Moor, the largest battle fought on English soil, could have been the final death blow for the Royalists but the opportunity to crush the other Royalist armies completely was not taken. The Scots went off to besiege the port of Newcastle, Fairfax engaged in mopping up operations against individual strongholds, while the Earl of Manchester returned to the East.

PROBLEMS FACING BOTH SIDES

Localism. Throughout the first two years of the war both sides were plagued with 'localism' – the reluctance of troops raised in one area to move far from home. Even the London Trained Bands were anxious to return after the

The Marquess of Newcastle.

relief of Gloucester and Hopton's steady Cornish Trained Bands had no wish to campaign in Hampshire. Also, money raised locally was often spent locally, rather than on armies in the field. Probably less than 10 per cent of monies raised by the Parliamentary county committees ever left their county. Even the Eastern Association, the most successful organisation in uniting county war efforts, was not immune from this.

Problems of disagreements and command structure. Both sides also suffered from a lack of coordinated command. Individual commanders tended to do their own thing.

- **Royalists.** In theory the Royalist war effort should have been more coordinated as Charles was Commander-in-Chief but, in a mirror of his Court in the period before 1642, faction and rivalries undermined the common cause. Digby did his best to turn Charles against his field commanders, especially Rupert. Some Royalist officers such as Lord George Goring did not always obey orders.
- **Parliament.** After 1643 the Parliamentary army was, in theory, under the command of the Committee of Two Kingdoms. In practice Parliamentary commanders would ignore their urgings. Both Essex and Manchester made their own decisions and the politicians had to live with them.

Thus neither side, at this stage, had a coordinated grand strategy being carried out by a national military machine. This, of course, was one of the main reasons why the First Civil War lasted so long.

The Royalist recovery. On the Parliamentary side, then, problems meant that the victory of Marston Moor was thrown away. Essex and Waller were supposed to advance on Oxford together but their rivalries meant that they could not cooperate for long, and Essex decided to take his army into the Royalist strongholds of the west of England where Lyme Regis was still holding out for Parliament. Meanwhile, Charles defeated Waller at Cropredy Bridge on 6 June. Waller's army disintegrated and the King pursued Essex into the west, defeating him at Lostwithiel in Cornwall. Essex's cavalry escaped and the infantry,

Sir William Waller.

KEY PERSON

Sir William Waller
Commander of Parliamentary forces in the south and west, a competent soldier, he had some victories but was defeated at Roundway Down in July 1643. He stopped Hopton's advance in Sussex in late 1643–early 1644. He was one of those who proposed the creation of the New Model army.

although disarmed, were so badly treated by the Royalists that many of them, once they reached Parliamentary territory again, voluntarily rejoined the army that Essex, who had escaped by sea, had formed.

The Earl of Manchester's failure. In October the Parliamentarians again missed an opportunity when the Royalists should have been destroyed but Manchester failed to chase them as they retreated after the second Battle of Newbury.

THE CREATION OF THE NEW MODEL ARMY, WINTER 1644

These failures led to a reorganisation that would finally overcome the problems of localism and lack of unified command. Cromwell accused Manchester of not wanting to win the war, and raised the fear in Parliament that, unless new measures and new commanders were put in place, the war would go on for ever. The result of this was the polite removal of Essex and Manchester and the creation, in the winter of 1644, of the New Model army of 22,000 men under the command of **Sir Thomas Fairfax**, with Cromwell commanding the cavalry. It was paid by Parliament, not by any local organisations, and from the beginning Fairfax and Cromwell insisted on tight discipline. The really reliable element was the old Eastern Association cavalry – the 'Ironsides' – but gradually professionalism and discipline took hold in the infantry too.

The New Model army
Formed in the winter of 1644, it was composed of elements of nearly all the Parliamentary armies. At first derided by Royalists as 'the new noddle', the New Model army was to become the most formidable professional army in Europe.

- **Cavalry.** At first the most effective element was the cavalry, largely drawn from the old Eastern Association – the 'Ironsides' trained by Cromwell – but gradually the whole army gained discipline and coherence.

- **Commanders.** The commanders were Sir Thomas Fairfax in overall command with Oliver Cromwell commanding the cavalry and Philip Skippon, a professional soldier who had fought in the Thirty Years War, commanding the infantry. Fairfax's and Cromwell's military skills are well known but Skippon has been rather overshadowed by them. He was a highly principled Puritan, a talented trainer of infantry as well as an inspiring leader. One captain said of him: 'never did I see any man so patient, so humble and so truly wise and valiant in all his actions'.
- **Promotion.** Its policy of promotion by merit was revolutionary and led to the rise of officers from humble backgrounds – a fact that caused both Royalists such as Hyde and socially conservative Parliamentarians such as Holles much concern. Holles remarked that 'most of the Colonels and Officers are mean tradesmen . . . a notable

KEY PERSON

Sir Thomas Fairfax
1621–71 Both Sir Thomas and his father Fernando, Lord Fairfax, fought for Parliament. At the beginning of the Civil War in Yorkshire, Sir Thomas already had some military experience in the Thirty Years War. For two years he fought a brilliant campaign in the north, including commanding the right wing of the Parliamentary forces at Marston Moor. After his appointment as Captain General of the New Model army in February 1645 he led it to final victory against the Royalists. He was not a politician and seems to have kept out of the political struggles of 1647, except to side with his troops over the question of arrears of pay. In 1648 during the Second Civil War he put down the Royalist risings in Kent and Essex. He refused to serve on the jury to try Charles I and in 1650 resigned rather than fight the Scots. During the 1650s he retired to his estates but supported the Restoration of Charles II in 1660. Personally brave, always having the welfare of the men he commanded as a priority, he had a strong bond with his soldiers.

Sir Thomas Fairfax.

dunghill if one would rake into it'. In fact the majority of the senior officers were, and remained in the future, from gentry families. Fairfax, Cromwell, Skippon, Lambert and Fleetwood were all from this social stratum, although it is true that some of the prominent colonels were tradesmen.

- **Religious independence.** It was not only its alleged social composition that raised alarm bells but its religious flavour. Independency, hostile to both Anglicanism and Presbyterianism, spread rapidly in the ranks of the cavalry especially, and the majority of all the officers could be regarded as **Independents**.

KEY THEME

Independents believed in religious toleration, i.e. that no one should be forced to attend Church. They believed in 'self-governing' congregations that would choose their own minister.

The New Model army at the Battle of Naseby, 1645

In June 1645 after Rupert, who had been conducting a brilliant cavalry campaign in the Midlands for some time, had captured and (of course) sacked Leicester, the King's main army was caught by the New Model army at Naseby in Northamptonshire. Again, as at Marston Moor, the advantage in ground and numbers lay with the Parliamentarians and again Rupert managed to smash the cavalry opposite him on the left. But, as usual, the Royalist cavalry did not wait for any further orders but charged away to capture the Parliamentary luggage train. Rupert, a brilliant, dashing commander had one dangerous fault: he never saw the importance of discipline *after* the first charge. Cromwell did. The Ironsides smashed the opposing Royalists on the right and then came to help the infantry in their battle with the Royalist infantry. The Royalists were completely destroyed and the King had lost his last field army capable of fighting a major pitched battle.

After that the New Model army was fighting a series of 'mopping up' operations against smaller Royalist forces, such as Goring's at Langport, and drawn-out sieges of Royalist strongholds. In March 1646, Sir Jacob Astley, the courageous commander of what was left of the Royalist infantry, surrendered at Stow-on-the-Wold. The King surrendered to the Scots in May and the last Royalist stronghold, Oxford, surrendered in June 1646.

Armour for light cavalry.

The Battle of Naseby.

CONCLUSION – WHY DID PARLIAMENT WIN THE CIVIL WAR?

- Greater financial resources in the East and South of England.
- Possession of London and East Anglia – trade and wealth.
- Rather better organisation of the above financial resources due to Pym's talents.
- King's strategic failures in 1642–3 when he still had some real chance of victory.
- Parliamentary control of the sea – prevented arms/troops reaching the King from abroad.
- The Solemn League and Covenant – Scottish help in the North of England.
- Eventual creation of central command structure and New Model army.

SUMMARY QUESTION

1 What were the military strengths of the Parliamentary side in the Civil War?

CHAPTER 5

Political and religious developments and the years of revolution, 1642–9

THE POLITICAL HISTORY OF THE CIVIL WAR, 1642–6

In Parliament

The Parliament that faced the King in the Civil War was not a united body; there were three 'parties' whose attitudes shaped the way Parliament fought the war – the 'Peace Party', the 'Middle Party' and the 'War Party'. To use the term 'party' might imply well-organised groups with clear leadership and clear programmes. This would be misleading; these three parties were loose groupings of 'like-minded gentry'.

- **The Peace Party.** The Peace Party was led by Denzil Holles and composed of those who had been the most reluctant to fight the King. They were always hoping for a settlement, and most of them only wanted the end of the Anglican Church rather than further restraints on the King's powers.
- **The Middle Party.** The Middle Party was led by **Pym** and was the largest group in 1642–3. They broadly stuck to the Nineteen Propositions (see page 31) but always hoped that the King would see reason and that a negotiated settlement could be found.
- **The War Party.** The War Party grew as the war dragged on. They tended to take a harder line about negotiations with the King, believing that he would not see reason and negotiate meaningfully unless he was defeated. Once defeated, real negotiations could begin from a position of strength. The leading lights of the War Party were Sir Henry Vane and Sir Arthur Heselrige, both future republicans. It would be a mistake, however, to see all those who supported the War Party, especially after 1643, as being 'radical'. Many MPs just wanted the war

Pym's skill in holding the different parties together
These 'parties' were held together by Pym until his death in December 1643. His policy of attempting to negotiate with the King, while setting up the financial and administrative machinery to win the war, meant that MPs of all opinions could usually be persuaded to support his measures.

finished off as quickly as possible before the country bled to death.

Pym's organisation of Parliament's finances for war. In February 1643 the assessments system was set up. Each county under Parliamentary control paid a tax, ironically similar to ship money, organised through County Committees. Compulsory loans were introduced in May 1643 and earlier, in April, fines were put upon Royalist supporters in Parliamentary areas and their estates were confiscated. They could only regain them by 'compounding': paying a heavy fine based on the value of the estate.

Pym's ruthless financial policies actually provided Parliament with enough money to fight the war, despite the County Committees often hanging on to money raised and using it for the defence of their own areas when it should have gone to the central war effort.

Manpower. Men as well as money were a priority; in August 1643 an **impressment ordinance** was passed. By 1645 at least half of Parliament's forces were people who were forced to fight. It is a measure of Pym's control of Parliament that such radical measures could be passed. Pym was helped by the failure of the negotiations with the King in the spring of 1643, when he was based at Oxford. Once it was clear that the King was not in a mood for compromise even most of the Peace Party reluctantly accepted Pym's measures.

The Solemn League and Covenant. By the autumn of 1643 Pym was a dying man, suffering from cancer. His last service to the Parliamentary cause was a military alliance with the Presbyterian Scots. This was the Solemn League and Covenant ratified on 7 September. The Scots' price for military help was the establishment of a Presbyterian Church settlement in England after victory. Many English MPs were less than enthusiastic about this prospect but, given the need for such help, decided to bide their time before opposing it, or watering it down from the intolerant version of Presbyterianism of their new allies.

The effect of the Cessation

Again, the King had made things easier for Pym, who could be accused of bringing in foreign help, by his own negotiations with the Catholic Irish rebels. These resulted in the Cessation of September 1643 (see page 41), which released Royal troops who had fought the Irish rebels for service with the King in England. Even more damagingly, the Irish Catholic confederates granted Charles £30,000. This only confirmed the view of many Englishmen about the King's fondness for popery. At least the Scots were fellow Protestants.

Pym's achievements

Pym died in December 1643. One historian has described the years 1640–3 as the reign of 'King Pym', as he completely dominated Parliament between these years.

- He had been the driving force behind Parliamentary opposition to the King since the Short Parliament of May 1640.
- He had been Parliament's virtually undisputed leader when the machinery of Personal Rule and Laudian control of the Church had been destroyed during 1641, and Parliament had followed the Nineteen Propositions with a shooting war largely at his prompting.
- He had then set up the machinery to win the war and, most remarkable of all, had held together the various shifting coalitions within Parliament.

Divisions after the death of Pym

- **War and Peace parties.** The split between the Peace Party and the War Party grew during 1644 while the Middle Party, the vast mass of MPs who had supported Pym, virtually ceased to exist. The majority of MPs moved towards the War Party's position.
- **Religious issues.** There was another potential faultline under the surface: that between Presbyterianism and the Independents. Independency had been a growing force in the country at large since 1642, helped by the collapse of Church authority. Presbyterians were a clear majority in Parliament but Independent MPs were gaining in numbers and influence. On many political issues Presbyterians and Independents could agree, and it

would be a mistake to assume that Presbyterians tended automatically to be more conservative, but there was a potential split which would show itself when a final Church settlement would have to be made.

- **The quarrel between Manchester and Cromwell.** The undercurrents of division between War Party and Peace Party, and between 'hard-line' Presbyterians and Independents, were to surface in the autumn of 1644. Manchester was an intolerant hard-line Presbyterian inclined to the Peace Party, so his conduct of operations against the King was less than dynamic. He was fighting to bring the King to terms, not to defeat him. Cromwell, the cavalry commander, was the hero of the War Party; he seemed to be the one commander with the drive and military competence to win the war. His relations with Manchester rapidly deteriorated in the summer of 1644. The **quarrel between Manchester and Cromwell** was eventually fought out in the House of Commons, and the result was a defeat for the Peace Party. The majority of MPs voted to remove Manchester, Essex and the other Parliamentary commanders by passing a 'Self-Denying Ordinance' on 3 April 1645: no member of either House of Parliament could hold a commission in the army. This was a face-saving device to remove Manchester and Essex without charging them with incompetence. Significantly, one MP was granted a dispensation to continue in his command – Oliver Cromwell.

The New Model army was then set up on 17 February 1645 and the victory of the War Party over the Peace Party seemed complete. Many of those who voted for the Self-Denying Ordinance and the setting up of the New Model army were formerly members of the moderate Middle Party. It was not that these men had become sympathetic to Independency or wanted to move harsh measures against the King, but the failure of the negotiations with Charles had further strengthened their fears that the war would go on for ever. A long war meant high taxes, social discontent, collapse of trade and perhaps collapse of traditional authority, so many of the War Party were conservatives trying to end a war, not radicals wanting to crush the King.

KEY THEME

The quarrel between Manchester and Cromwell

Cromwell's style of warfare and his determination to beat the King disturbed Manchester who remarked: 'If we beat the King ninety and nine times yet he is King still . . . but if the King beat us once we shall all be hanged and our posterity made slaves'. Cromwell's reply was typical: 'If this be so, why did we take up arms at first? This is against fighting ever hereafter.' Cromwell seemed to Manchester and his Parliamentarian allies to be a dangerous radical with his policy of promotion by merit rather than birth. Also his promotion and protection of Independents made it seem as if he were building up the influence of Independents within the army.

The end of the war

When the war finally ended in the summer of 1646 the War Party ceased to have any meaning. The King was beaten and, at the same time, threatening social, religious and political undercurrents were surfacing outside Westminster. So the basic conservatism of the majority of MPs reasserted itself: the MPs were radical in neither religion nor politics – they expected now the war was won to be able to negotiate a settlement with the King.

RELIGIOUS AND POLITICAL DEVELOPMENTS OUTSIDE PARLIAMENT, 1642–8

In many ways the war created a much more complicated religious and political situation:

- The collapse of the authority of the Church meant that more unorthodox religious views began to spread.
- The end of censorship caused a great outpouring of pamphlet literature on both religious and political ideas. Although perhaps only one person in five could read, pamphlets were read out to those who could not.
- The Parliamentary army became a hotbed of new religious and political ideas: for the first time such ideas could spread easily among a lot of people gathered together.
- The war itself meant a collapse of the traditional rule in the countryside; the gentry were often absent, the courts did not function regularly. In some ways, society was in danger of dissolving under the stress of war.

Religion

Independents. The most important development was the spread of **Independency**. Independents were opposed by both Anglicans and Presbyterians because, whatever their differences, they believed in one state church to which all should belong. The Independents believed in some form of national church but without powers to make people attend that church. Independency grew before the Civil War, being strongest in East Anglia, and it spread through the Parliamentary army from the cavalry of the Eastern Association. Its patron was Oliver Cromwell, and by 1646

KEY THEME

Independency in the army
Richard Baxter, a Presbyterian minister, had this experience of the army in 1644: 'But when I came to the army, among Cromwell's soldiers, I found a new face of things which I never dreamed of. I heard the plotting heads very hot upon that which intimated their intention to subvert both the church and State . . . Independency and Anabaptistry were most prevalent . . . I perceived that they took the King for a tyrant and an enemy . . . they said what were the Lords of England but William the Conqueror's Colonels, and the Barons but his Majors, or the Knights but his Captains'.

Independency was challenging Parliamentary Presbyterianism.

The sects. Far more radical were the sects. Like Independents they believed in a 'gathered church' of like-minded members but rejected any idea of state church organisation.

- The most popular of the sects were the Baptists (often called Anabaptists) who believed in adult baptism but were fairly conventional in their other religious ideas. Some sects, however, were far more radical.
- The Fifth Monarchists were convinced of the imminent coming of Christ, that there had been four monarchies prophesied in Scripture and the Fifth Monarchy would be the reign of 'King Jesus'. They were to be a significant force in the early 1650s, a force out of all proportion to their size.
- Some sects, such as the Ranters and the Muggletonians, had few members and often preached that 'sin was not sin unless the sinner thought it was'.

There was a degree of what could only be called religious mania developing by 1646, with tiny sects all claiming to have the absolute truth and sending shivers down the spines of Presbyterians and even some Independents.

Politics

The Civil War had started as a political and religious argument between the King and Parliament – the aristocracy and gentry. However, as the war went on, some of the 'lower orders' – the classes below the gentry – began to stir and think politically, and to take action.

Some action was purely self-defence, as in the case of the **Clubmen**. In the increasing anarchy of the war, country people, in the West particularly, organised their districts into defensive pacts. Tired of looting troops, they were determined to resist troops from either side entering their territory. Interestingly they were not organised by the gentry, as the failed neutrality pacts of 1642–3 had been. These were farmers, cottagers and artisans practising self-help. They may not have been very successful but they

KEY TERM

Clubmen By 1644 many of the ordinary people in the countryside were heartily sick of soldiers living for free, destroying their crops and terrorising their neighbourhoods. They formed themselves into groups called Clubmen, determined to keep all troops out of their neighbourhood.

showed that these sort of people could act independently of their gentry 'masters'. They also highlighted the slide towards anarchy that was occurring.

The Levellers. The most important political development outside Parliament was the rise of the Levellers. **Leveller ideas** had first circulated in London, in pamphlet form. The main pamphleteers were **John Lilburne**, William Walwyn and Richard Overton. It would be a mistake, however, to see these as 'leaders' in the modern political sense. The Levellers were not a well-organised political party with a clear leadership structure. Their ideas, sometimes modified, had spread in London but it was the army that was to be most influenced by, and influential in, Levellerism. Radical religious ideas had been spreading, with unauthorised preaching, and some of these radical religious ideas became entwined, for some, with radical political ideas.

The radicals in politics were a small minority but the treatment of the army by Parliament in 1647 over arrears of pay played into their hands (see page 90). The Levellers had influence out of all proportion to their numbers but this was to be short-lived. The Levellers failed to force through the radical political programme that they put forward in the army debates at Putney in 1647 for the following reasons:

- The majority of the army trusted Cromwell, rather than the Leveller spokesmen.
- The majority were more interested in bread-and-butter issues, such as pay and indemnity for acts carried out under orders during the war, rather than paper constitutions.
- The Levellers, as already noted, had no clear leadership or organisational structure.
- Their most dynamic army representative Colonel Rainborough was killed in the Second Civil War.
- Cromwell put down the Leveller mutinies at Corkbush (1647) and Burford (1649) very rapidly before they could get out of hand.

Nevertheless, vaguely Leveller ideas of radical reform continued to circulate throughout the years up to the

KEY THEME

Leveller ideas

- In the state of nature all men were naturally free and equal.

- Englishmen were free in the past and had been enslaved by the Norman Conquest – 'The Norman Yoke'.

- As all were equal in the sight of God, so they should be in society.

- The electoral system should be reformed so that there would be equal electoral districts.

- All men over 21 should vote. Some Levellers wished to exclude servants and those receiving alms (local charity), as they would not be independent voters.

John Lilburne.

*Gaze not upon this shaddow that is vaine.
But rather raise thy thoughts a higher Straine.
To GOD (I meane) who set this young-man free.
And in like Straits can eke deliuer thee.*

John Lilburne

Most of the leading Levellers who published Leveller ideas were not in the army. The most prominent Leveller was John Lilburne. He had already been imprisoned before the Civil War in 1638 for publishing attacks on the bishops. Released by the Long Parliament, at Cromwell's suggestion, he later joined the Parliamentary army, leaving in 1645 rather than sign the Covenant – the agreement to become a Presbyterian (unlike the Independents who signed but had no intention of keeping to it). He then started to write attacks on the Presbyterian majority in Parliament. Later in 1645 he published his famous first Leveller pamphlet – *England's Birthright Justified* – which called for free speech and annual parliaments. Briefly imprisoned by the House of Lords, he took no part in the Putney Debates. He later opposed the Rump and was again imprisoned. Lilburne had played some part in drawing up the Leveller programme of 1647, but he was an individualist and a showman, not a leader of a political movement. His fellow Leveller authors, William Walwyn and Richard Overton, probably did more to put Leveller ideas clearly in the pamphlets and proposals of 1647.

Restoration, and some of the junior officers still had hopes of radical reforms throughout this period. Levellerism as a threat to the regimes of the period between 1649 and 1660, however, was not very significant.

THE YEARS OF REVOLUTION, 1646–9

Introduction

There are some main themes to these years which are crucial to understanding the events:

- **The 'conservative' Parliamentary gentry lose control.** The essential element is how the gentry, who had gone to war in 1642 to bring Charles to an understanding of the traditional constitution (as they saw it), lost control

of the situation with the result that a series of events which, for the traditional 'political nation', were shocking, and indeed unthinkable, took place.

- **The execution of the King.** The trial and execution of the King in revolutionary style as an enemy of the people, the destruction of the old constitution with the abolition of the House of Lords and kingship itself with the establishment of a Republic – 'the Commonwealth of England'.

- **The Commonwealth and the army.** This was to lead to the rule of a small 'unrepresentative' group, and the emergence of a new interest group – the army. Despite the army's power and influence it could never really bring itself to rule as a military regime. Instead it tried to create a 'civilian' government which would be sympathetic to its wishes.

With the defeat of the King's main field army at Naseby, the end of the Civil War was in sight. The surrender of the last major position of the King's army at Stow-on-the-Wold was memorable for the telling remark of the old soldier, commander of the King's infantry, Sir Jacob Astley: 'You have done your work boys and may go and play unless you fall out amongst yourselves.'

The differences between those who had supported or fought for Parliament in the First Civil War had been evident by 1644. Cromwell and his Independent associates in the army had been objects of suspicion to the more conservative Peace Party Presbyterians, such as Holles and Manchester, who had lost the political battle for the control of the army to Cromwell and Fairfax in the Parliamentary debates of 1644.

The War Party. The War Party in Parliament had been dominant in 1644–5. They had but a single idea – win the war first then negotiate with Charles from a position of strength.

- The War Party's support for Cromwell and Fairfax and their consequent establishment of the New Model army was *not* intended to defeat and then humiliate, or even execute, the King.

- Regicide (killing the king) was simply unthinkable for the vast majority of MPs and was not an issue in 1646. The issue was to win a war that had dragged on for too long. Many of them had the awful example of the Thirty Years War in Germany in front of them.
- Once the war was won, they believed that Charles would surely see the logic of his position and come to terms.
- Therefore, many of the War Party in the Commons were neither radical in religion nor in politics. Their fear was the creeping anarchy that a continuing war, without victory, would bring. They were worried that England would simply collapse into chaos.

Hopes for peace. When that victory came the War Party virtually ceased to exist. They assumed that Charles would now negotiate in good faith because he had been defeated. In these circumstances leadership of the House of Commons passed to the opponents of the Independents and army men in Parliament. MPs now aimed to come rapidly to an agreement with the King, disband the hideously expensive and increasingly threatening army, and establish a national Presbyterian Church which all people would have to attend.

The reality of 1646. To understand what happened in the next three years it is necessary to understand why, probably from the beginning, this was far too optimistic a programme based on several false beliefs. These were that:

- the army could be dispensed with, without paying its full arrears of pay;
- the King would negotiate in good faith;
- Independency both in the army and in a minority in Parliament could be suppressed or ignored.

Denzil Holles.

The leadership of Denzil Holles. The chief believer in these false ideas was Denzil Holles, the Peace Party leader of 1642. By 1646 Holles was speaking, and acting, for the naturally conservative majority of the House of Commons.

The changed political situation
The beliefs held in 1642 among the moderate gentry of Parliament no longer operated by 1646–7.

- Firstly, the army would not automatically obey Parliament. Most soldiers in the infantry had been conscripted and probably would have been happy to be 'paid off', but a significant majority had had their ideas fundamentally changed by the experience of soldiering in this unique army.
- Cromwell had introduced a policy of promotion by merit. This was a truly revolutionary idea in a time when everyone believed in keeping to their own social class and respecting those who were of a higher social class. Promotion by merit had produced officers from humble backgrounds, who were now accustomed to giving orders rather than taking them from their social betters as they had in civilian life.
- Independency had spread among the literate soldiers. This process had, of course, been encouraged by Cromwell's promotion of Independents, already opposed by Manchester in 1644. Independency, with its implicit denial of Church authority, encouraged its supporters to think for themselves. Some made the jump from independent thought in religion to independent political thought. In 1647 radical political ideas were to find a ready audience among these newly 'freed' soldiers. These were the men who had won the war – why should they tamely go home and allow the traditional rulers of the countryside to reassert their control over them? Of course, it was only a minority of the New Model army who came gradually to think like this. But it was enough to make the army a new force in politics – a force that had not existed in 1642 and a force without whose agreement no settlement could be reached.

The King's attitudes to a settlement

The King was another element in this increasingly fragmented situation.

- Far from seeing the logic of his position, he had no intention of giving up any of his powers and prerogatives.
- He saw himself as central to any agreement; he could not conceive a situation where he was not the key figure to be negotiated with and his agreement sought.

- As far as Charles was concerned all his enemies – Parliament, the army, the Presbyterians, the Independents, the Scots – were traitors.
- It followed to Charles, that any agreements with these people could be broken and that his only duty was to regain his rightful God-given place as a divine-right monarch.
- To Charles there was no difference between Denzil Holles and Oliver Cromwell. He had no intention of making a binding agreement with anybody. The longer he prolonged the negotiations, the more his enemies would 'fall out amongst themselves', the greater the chance of anarchy and therefore a reaction in favour of the traditional ruler who represented law and order.

Religious divisions

The Presbyterians loathed and feared Independency. To them Independents represented a potentially anarchical system of church government. Anglicanism was wrong but so was the idea of the gathered congregation. Any agreement with Charles must include the establishment of the Presbyterian religion as the *state* religion, giving it the power to crush both Anglicans and the increasingly diffuse Independent congregations.

Had Independency not had a power base in the army then perhaps this would have been a realistic aim. Independents were in the minority in the country and in Parliament, but the army gave them a strength that the Presbyterians in Parliament quite failed to grasp.

SUMMARY QUESTIONS

1 What do you think was the most serious division on the Parliamentary side? Explain your answer fully.

2 Why were the Independents such a significant section of the army?

CHAPTER 6

Background to the Second Civil War and regicide

THE SPLIT BETWEEN PARLIAMENT AND THE ARMY, 1646–8

Introduction

Many MPs led by Denzil Holles wanted to get rid of the army as soon as possible as they saw it as a threat to their position. The army wanted an Independent religious settlement and some of the army actually wanted to influence the negotiations with the King. Holles did not offer the army a reasonable financial settlement to encourage them to disband and go home. Therefore the army began to see that the only way they could get what they saw as their rights was to interfere in any settlement with the King.

The Solemn Engagement

The army, thoroughly disillusioned with Holles and the Presbyterian majority in Parliament, held a rendezvous at Newmarket on 29 May 1647 where the 'Solemn Engagement' was approved. The Engagement declared:

- the army would not disband until they had received a settlement that would have the approval of an Army Council;
- this Council would represent the opinions of all parts of the army because it was to be composed of the general officers of the army, two commissioned officers from each regiment and two soldiers from each regiment.

Now the army were asserting their rights, as a body acting together, to defy the Parliament that had created them.

Parliament's offers to Charles

At Uxbridge in 1645 the King refused to accept a 'Presbyterian' settlement because the Royalist Marquess of

The pay of the army By 1647 the infantry were owed 18 weeks' pay; the cavalry 43 weeks'. Insultingly, Holles offered only 6 weeks' pay or service in Ireland. It was largely this treatment that caused the army to unite against Parliament.

Montrose (later to be defeated) was still having successes for the Royalists in Scotland.

The King's negotiations with Parliament. While a prisoner of the Scots before they handed him to Parliament in exchange for payment of the Scottish army, Charles received the **Newcastle Propositions**. Charles played for time, eventually accepting a modified form of the Propositions, or appearing to do so.

- This agreement could have opened out the prospect of a new coalition of forces against the army – a coalition of the Presbyterians in Parliament, the Royalists and the Scots.
- The Scots had entered the war on the side of Parliament in 1643 to ensure the victory of Presbyterianism, so could now support the King against the Independent-dominated army which they feared and disliked as much as Holles and his Parliamentary colleagues did.

The army and a settlement

The army's reaction to this potential new alliance was to take steps to ensure that they would be a main player in settlement negotiations with the King, while neutralising the potential threat that this coalition posed. Cornet Joyce, with 500 troops, went to Holdenby on 2 June, seized the King and brought him to the army at Newmarket. The army could now negotiate with the King directly.

The Declaration of the Army. The Declaration of the Army followed, saying that they were: 'No mere mercenary army hired to serve any arbitrary power of a State, but called for, and conjured by the several declarations of Parliament, to the defence of our own and the people's just rights and liberties.' The Declaration demanded that Parliament set a date for its own dissolution and be purged of 'delinquent or corrupt members'. These were, of course, the leading Presbyterian opponents of the army. Eleven were 'impeached' in the name of the army (not, of course, that the army had any legal standing to do this) and, because there was a clear threat that the army would march on London, these members withdrew from Parliament.

So by June 1647 the possibility of a slide into anarchy seemed closer. To all intents and purposes there were three different 'centres of authority' each claiming the right to arbitrate a settlement – the King, Parliament and the army. The King's hope that his opponents would 'fall out amongst themselves' appeared to be realised.

The Heads of Proposals – the army's offer to the King. The Council of the army had formulated the Heads of Proposals, and these were put to the King by Cromwell and Henry Ireton, the Commissary General. **Charles prolonged the negotiations**, perhaps making two errors:

- Firstly, regarding religion, the Heads were, in some ways, the best offer for a King who said that one of his main principles was the protection of the Anglican Church. Previous Parliamentary offers had all meant the destruction of the Anglican Church; because Presbyterianism would become the state religion enforced by law, no other religions would be allowed. The Heads of Proposals involved religious toleration, so by implication the Church of England could exist. Charles could be an Anglican but the Church would have no coercive powers; it would not be able to force people to attend its services.
- Secondly, the army actually had the power to enforce a settlement. Parliament could not come to an agreement with the King that the army would not accept, because they could, given their military strength, quite simply block it. Ultimate power now lay not with civilian Parliamentarians but with the army, if the army held together. Charles failed to see the simple point that 'power grows out of the barrel of a gun'.

'Counter-revolution' in London

A new development forced its way into this complex situation on 26 July. A Presbyterian 'counter-revolutionary' coup took place in London. A mob, possibly organised by Holles, invaded the House of Commons and the House of Lords. Throughout this period there were two mobs that could be raised in London – a 'conservative' one and a 'radical' one – and it was the former that had the upper hand. They attacked Members of Parliament who were

Charles's attitude Charles continued to believe that he had more power than he actually had. His remark to Ireton is revealing: 'You cannot be without me; you will fall to ruin if I do not sustain you.' The army leaders soon became disillusioned with what they saw as Charles's attitude and his attempts to widen differences between his opponents. Ireton said: 'Sir, you have the intention to be an arbitrator between the Parliament and us, and we mean it to be between Your Majesty and Parliament' – thus neatly summing up the lack of understanding of the situation that Charles had. Typically, Charles regarded the army leaders as men of no principle, as he regarded all who had fought against him. He blamed the failure of the negotiations on the fact that he had not offered Cromwell and Ireton peerages.

disposed to come to an agreement with the army, they restored the eleven Presbyterians who had withdrawn from Parliament, and forced the Commons to pass a resolution inviting the King to come to London, despite the fact that, under arrest by the army, he was in no position to do so. The leading Independent members, who were the allies of the army, then fled to it.

The response of the army. The response of the army was swift; they occupied London on 6 August. They hoped not only to keep down the 'counter-revolutionary' elements but also to put some pressure on Parliament to accept the basic ideas of the Declaration and the Heads. Given the composition of Parliament this was not likely.

Potential splits in the army

By October 1647 many of the junior officers and rank and file were becoming disillusioned with the failure of Parliament to move on the demands made earlier in the summer. Also, with the continuing negotiations with the King not bearing any fruit, the senior officers came under suspicion from the same elements in the army who regarded the senior officers as 'grandees', potentially selling out by being unwilling to force Parliament or the King to a settlement.

'The Case of the Army Truly Stated'. This feeling of frustration with Parliament and the King, combined with an unease about the role of the likes of Cromwell and Ireton, fed radical and Leveller ideas. These ideas, around for some time, became influential, surfacing in 'The Case of the Army Truly Stated' which demanded not only biennial parliaments (elections every two years) but that 'all free born Englishmen over 21 should vote' and that 'all power is originally . . . in the whole body of the people'.

Putney Debates. These were remarkable debates held in Putney Church. The Levellers in the army discussed with the senior officers what the future constitution of England should be. The representatives of each regiment – known as 'agitators' – were ranged against Cromwell and Ireton. The more conservative political instincts of the latter would not allow them to consider such sweeping reforms

KEY PERSON

Henry Ireton From a gentry family, he fought with Cromwell throughout 1643–6 and married Cromwell's daughter. Ireton was the main thinker behind the Heads of Proposals; a clear political thinker opposed to the very radical ideas of the Levellers. He organised Pride's Purge which led to the trial of the King, and died in 1651 in Ireland.

Henry Ireton.

as the Levellers put forward in the first 'Agreement of the People'.

'The Agreement of the People'. This continued the arguments put forward in 'The Case of the Army Truly Stated'. It demanded that:

* there be biennial parliaments;
* no authority was above Parliament;
* nobody could be forced to do military service;
* all should be equal in the eyes of the law;

- parliamentary constituencies should be of the same size (this would get rid of many of the seats which had only a few people voting and would give more seats to areas where people were not so well represented);
- the present Parliament should be dissolved on 31 December 1648.

The senior officers' reaction to the Levellers. Cromwell opposed Leveller ideas on the grounds that they would lead to anarchy. Ireton, a clearer political thinker, took a more philosophical stance in the discussions. He argued against the Leveller idea of 'natural rights', and took the view that society was based upon property. The argument that natural rights determined how society should be organised meant that property would disappear, because if the propertyless were allowed to vote they would create a Parliament that would take property away from property holders. In Ireton's reasoning those without property could not be trusted to act responsibly because they had nothing to lose. Therefore, he argued, only those who had 'a permanent fixed interest in the Kingdom' should vote.

The Levellers' attitudes in the Putney Debates. One of the most radical of the Levellers, **Colonel Thomas Rainborough**, stood on the idea of 'natural rights', arguing that 'the poorest he that is in England hath a life to live as the greatest he' and that all should vote. **John Wildman**, another prominent radical, argued that although the soldiers had no property to risk in the war that had just been fought they had risked their lives and therefore that was their 'stake in the country'. By fighting they had earned the right to vote.

Failure to come to an agreement. The opposing views of the senior officers and the Levellers could not be reconciled, although Cromwell was anxious to keep the army together, fearing anarchy if it were to fall apart in arguments. He stressed what they all agreed on – some kind of reform and religious toleration – but his sympathies on the subject of really radical political reforms were with Ireton and the other 'grandees'.

Introduction

The Second Civil War was in essence a series of uprisings, often with local grievances, as much as Royalist sympathies, as the driving force. Some Presbyterians joined the Royalists, most remained neutral, as did the mass of the country, appalled by the prospect of another civil war.

Charles escapes

The debates were brought to an end by events outside the control of the army. On 11 November, Charles I escaped from army custody and allied himself with the Scots by the Engagement of 26 December. He also made contacts with English Royalists to organise risings. Parliament was, temporarily, as horrified by the implications of this as the army and passed a Vote of No Addresses: they would no longer negotiate with the King.

- It was obvious that a second civil war, with Charles, the Scots and Royalist elements ranged against the army and a very reluctant Parliament, was about to break out.
- In these circumstances Leveller agitation died down, with the exception of a mutiny at Corkbush Field which Cromwell put down easily. In the last resort the soldiers would trust Oliver Cromwell in dangerous times rather than the radicals, so the army was united again.

Effects of Charles's actions. Charles had also succeeded, temporarily, in uniting most of Parliament and the army, grandees and radicals alike, against him. There seems to have been a swing in public opinion in favour of Charles during late 1647 and he was counting on this as much as on the Scots and Royalists. However, he had put himself in a much more dangerous position should he lose the war.

The failure of the Royalists. The revolts in Kent, Essex, south Wales and Norwich were as much against high taxation, the hated County Committees and the army as they were for undiluted Royalism. Fanatical Royalists, such as Roger Le Strange, a Norfolk man who played a prominent and disastrous role in the Kent uprising, were not universally trusted by their allies. The risings were not well coordinated, nor did they attract the sort of mass support, as opposed to sympathy, that would have made them victorious against the army. There was some vicious fighting, especially at Colchester where executions took place after the fall of the town, but the army soon regained control. The Scottish invasion, perhaps the greatest threat, was halted by Cromwell in a brilliant action at Preston where he inflicted a crushing defeat in August 1648.

Charles himself had fled from Hampton Court to Carisbrooke Castle on the Isle of Wight. He believed that the governor Robin Hammond would be sympathetic and provide him with a secure base from which to organise the war. However, after some hesitation Hammond, Cromwell's cousin, imprisoned him – the secure base that would give the King freedom of action had become a trap.

THE TRIAL AND EXECUTION OF CHARLES I

Negotiations restart with the King

KEY THEME

Presbyterian reaction The Presbyterian majority in Parliament would never harm the King personally, but at the Windsor Prayer Meeting, held before the army went off to fight in March 1648, they swore to bring 'that man of blood, Charles Stuart to an account for the blood that he had shed'.

With the end of the Second Civil War, the gap between the conservative and moderate, largely **Presbyterian majority in Parliament** on one side and a minority of Independent MPs and the army on the other widened again. For the majority of MPs there could be no settlement without the King and the Vote of No Addresses was repealed. Negotiations started again with the Newport treaty. Parliament could not countenance the army's desire for religious toleration and obvious radical leanings, so a settlement with Charles was attractive, regardless of the past. The King, of course, continued to regard himself as indispensable.

The army's decision to try the King

The army felt differently. They were largely united in the view that there could be no peace while Charles lived and, furious at the repeal of the Vote of No Addresses, the decision was taken to try him. Probably Ireton was the driving force behind this. Parliament as it was then constituted would, of course, never agree to a trial. It would not only be totally illegal under the constitution,

The death warrant of Charles I.

but to their conservative instincts the trial of an anointed sovereign was simply unthinkable.

The army and the group of Independent MPs who were their allies could not, for their part, bring themselves simply to execute Charles. They had to justify themselves in the eyes of the world, so the trial of the King as a war criminal was essential, however dubious its legality. Some parliamentary element was needed to give the impression that the law was being observed – an army court martial would not do.

Pride's Purge. Therefore, on 6 December 1648 **Colonel Thomas Pride**, armed with a list of MPs whom the army were sure would never vote for a trial, stood at the door of the House of Commons. He kept out some 110 MPs, some being held in house arrest overnight. Another 250, seeing which way the wind was blowing, either withdrew or did not even attempt to enter. This left 60 or so members, including **Cromwell**, who would agree to a trial. Altogether 135 commissioners were named to try the King, only half of whom actually turned up.

Charles's conduct at the trial. Throughout the trial Charles refused to plead or speak, on the legal grounds that there was no law that could try him – he was the law. It is possible that Charles saw the trial as a bluff to try to force him into a settlement, completely misunderstanding his opponents once again. After Bradshaw, the presiding

KEY PERSON

Colonel Thomas Pride
Probably a former brewer's clerk who rose through Cromwell's policy of promotion by merit. His name is associated with the 'purge' of the House of Commons that left a 'rump' willing to vote for a trial of the King. He signed the King's death warrant and was a convinced republican. He died in 1658.

KEY THEME

Cromwell's attitude to the trial Characteristically, Cromwell, who was engaged in a 'mopping up' operation against Pontefract Castle when Pride's Purge occurred, seems to have been in two minds as to the advisability of a trial. But once his mind was made up he went through with it. The Dutch envoys who came to plead for Charles's life were told by Cromwell: 'We will cut off his head with the crown on it.'

The execution of Charles I.

judge, passed sentence of death he suddenly tried to speak for the first time, as if he finally realised that the trial was in earnest.

On 30 January 1649 Charles passed to the scaffold through a hole knocked in the wall of the Banqueting House in Whitehall. Thus one of the last sights that he saw on earth was that great piece of 'absolutist' architecture with its Rubens ceiling depicting his father passing up to heaven. It was a particularly apt venue for the final act, the execution of a King whose absolutist leanings, as much as his incompetence and lack of understanding of the forces ranged against him, had brought him to this final tragedy.

SUMMARY QUESTIONS

1 Why did Parliament and the army split after 1646?

2 Why, by 1649, had the army and some members of Parliament decided to try the king?

A2: ANALYSIS AND INTERPRETATION

SECTION 1

Causes of the Civil War

WHY BY 1640 WAS THE MAJORITY OF THE POLITICAL NATION OPPOSED TO ROYAL POLICIES?

Introduction

The formation of an 'anti-Court consensus' did not mean opposition to kingship or King Charles, it meant a deep-seated suspicion of his advisers and the tendency towards absolutism. Nearly all of the 'political nation' accepted that the King had prerogatives which were his by right, but the policies of the 1630s seemed to indicate that Charles did not understand the 'spirit' of the constitution, or that his subjects had rights too.

- It is important to understand that, in the 1630s, it was Charles, Laud and Strafford who were *seen* as the innovators, moving towards a continental-style absolutist monarchy. This was the trend all over Europe, where parliaments and the rights of individuals were being abolished and kings were becoming more and more powerful.
- Laud's religious policies seemed to be aimed at bringing in Roman Catholicism by the back door. The change in the position of the altar, raised up at the east end of the church, aimed to make the priest and communion more separate from the congregation. This seemed a move towards a more Catholic ritual, as was the 1633 Prayer Book. Laud's attacks on 'the ratsbane of lecturing' were seen as persecuting honest Protestant preachers – he saw them as Puritan fanatics and subversives. Bowing at the name of Jesus, the erection of images and other aspects of decoration in churches, and priestly vestments – intended to promote the 'beauty of holiness' – all seemed to be Roman Catholic in spirit. His determination to raise the status of the clergy also seemed to be a reassertion of the power of the Church to the position of authority it held in pre-Reformation times. Laud associated the Church with support for divine-right monarchy thus confirming the connection between Roman Catholicism and absolutism.
- Charles's financial policies – ship money, forest fines, distraint of knighthood – all seemed to be semi-legal and attacked property rights.

- The Scottish war against fellow Protestants was not only resented because there was sympathy for fellow Protestants oppressed by Laud, but it was also a failure.
- Strafford in Ireland had shown how Personal Rule might work and his appearance in England in 1639 was a frightening development.
- Charles's failure to call a Parliament for eleven years seemed to indicate that, if he could, he would never call another, and England would gradually become an absolutist state.
- Charles's 'pro-Spanish' foreign policy was viewed as part of the Roman Catholic/absolutist trend.

Therefore by 1640 the majority of the political nation had the gravest suspicions about the direction of Court policies. These suspicions came together in the belief in a Roman Catholic conspiracy to set up an absolutist continental-style monarchy and to abolish the constitution and the common law. There was a general feeling after the failure of the Short Parliament that Charles called the Long Parliament because he had to, not because he had moderated his policies. Therefore the calling of the Parliament did not, in the eyes of the country gentry, mean that the danger was over.

WHAT PART DID EVENTS IN SCOTLAND AND IRELAND PLAY IN CAUSING A CIVIL WAR?

Key themes
- As far as English politics are concerned, the elements which caused a crisis in 1640 and eventually led to a civil war in 1642 are, of course, the deep suspicions aroused by Charles's Personal Rule policies in the 1630s, and his failure to reassure a large element of the gentry in Parliament that he could be trusted to rule according to the 'old constitution'.
- The mutual suspicions and incomprehension in a period of crisis therefore drove events in England.
- However, it can be argued that the two turning points that led to the situation in 1642 were the result of events that happened in Charles's other two kingdoms, Scotland and Ireland.

The Scottish wars. The fall of Personal Rule was not the result of a revolt by the gentry, however unpopular Charles's policies, financial and religious, were. The fall of Personal Rule that forced Charles to call a Parliament in 1640 was directly caused by the Scottish wars. Laud's and Charles's disastrous policy of trying to force a 'High Church' Prayer Book on the strongly Puritan Scots in 1637 led to a revolt of his Scottish subjects. This was a revolt that, despite previous antipathies between the English gentry and the Scots, found some sympathy among the Puritan

English gentry. The ineffectiveness of English forces against the Scots was the result of not just an inefficient militia, ill-equipped and ill-trained, but a reluctance to fight 'fellow sufferers' of Laud's policies. Thus some troops, raised to fight the Scots, hanged their Roman Catholic officers and smashed down altar rails in churches before deserting at the first opportunity.

The Scots, of course, united behind the Presbyterian Covenant of 28 February 1638, were now directly challenging Charles's rule. The humiliating defeat after a skirmish near Kelso when the Covenanters, under the former professional soldier Sir Alexander Leslie, routed Charles's reluctant army, should have demonstrated to Charles that he had lost control of his northern kingdom, and that only negotiations on the basis of allowing the Scots to choose their own religion could prevent further disaster.

However, the Pacification of Berwick of June 1639 was seen by Charles merely as an armistice while he gathered fresh strength, money and forces. Both 'sides' should have disarmed but Charles had no intention of giving up what he saw as his God-given rights.

Strafford had advised Charles to call a Parliament, believing that traditional loyalty to the Crown and dislike of the Scots would ensure that what became known as the Short Parliament of May 1640 voted subsidies to bring the Scots to heel. Strafford, not long back from Ireland, was out of touch. Parliament refused to vote any money until Charles had dealt with their 'grievances'. The Short Parliament was dismissed and only Convocation, the Church assembled under Laud, provided Charles with money, as perhaps was to be expected. With Charles planning an attack on Scotland despite his difficulties, the Scots took the offensive and decisively defeated the Royal forces at Newburn on 28 August. The result of Newburn, and the **Treaty of Ripon** that followed, was decisive in its effects on English history.

The English were in no doubt as to why Charles had called the Long Parliament, and to whom they owed the end of Personal Rule. Robert Baillie, the Presbyterian Scottish negotiator, made clear that everyone owed their liberties, religion and Parliament to the Scottish army. Thus it can be argued that the train of events that led to the downfall of Personal Rule were directly caused by events in Scotland.

The problem was, of course, that many realised that Charles had not called Parliament because he had had a conversion to 'constitutional' ways and had decided to abandon Personal Rule as a mistaken policy, but because the Scots had forced him to. Thus the stage was set for the fears and suspicions of the next year. Parliament could not be sure that Charles

KEY EVENT

The Treaty of Ripon, October 1640. It enabled the Scots to occupy the six northern counties, being paid £850 per day while doing so. Significantly, the Scots also insisted that the Treaty, negotiated on the English side by a Council of Peers, should be ratified by an English Parliament. In any case, with the Scots sitting on London's vital coal supplies, which they could cut off at any time they wished, and with an empty Treasury, Charles had no choice but reluctantly to call Parliament in November.

was discussing and negotiating in good faith – he was doing it at the barrel of a gun.

What was the importance of the Irish Rebellion? If the Scottish revolt caused the calling of the Long Parliament, the Irish Rebellion created the final crisis that was to transform a situation of mutual suspicion and distrust into a crisis whose effects were to propel England into civil war. By the 1630s Ireland was a troubled and divided country. Henry VIII and Elizabeth had re-established English rule over the native Catholic Irish and their lords. The leading Catholic lords in Ireland, the Earls Tyrconnel and Tyrone, had fled abroad, allowing James I to seize their vast landholdings and create 'plantations' of Scottish and English Protestants. These had tended to be Presbyterian and were more hostile to the native Roman Catholic Irish than the tolerant Anglicans who already held land in Ireland.

So, there were three distinct groups in Ireland: the Gaelic Irish, feeling increasingly under threat from Protestant immigrants; the 'old ascendency', Anglo-Irish Anglican gentry, many of whom had been in Ireland for a very long time; and new 'plantation' Protestants.

Thomas Wentworth, later Earl of Strafford, appointed Lord Deputy in 1633, was determined to rule Ireland entirely as a 'province' of England regardless of the feelings of any of these groups. He reduced the Irish Parliament to a 'rubber stamp', alienated the 'old ascendancy' gentry by his high-handed methods, and sought to rule the Gaelic Catholics with an iron hand and an army raised in Ireland. He also supported the 'High Church' Laudian policies in Ireland against the tolerant Archbishop of Armagh, James Usher. When Strafford's iron hand was removed the Irish Parliament, Protestants all, watered down his measures. This weakened these measures in the eyes of the Gaelic Irish who were determined to halt the loss of their land to Protestants, especially in Ulster.

On 22 October 1641 the Gaelic Irish rose in revolt in Ulster. Massacres did take place but nothing on the scale which reports reaching the English Parliament suggested. The effect of the news of the rebellion (or massacre as it was called at the time) cannot be overestimated. The fact that by December Sir Phelim O'Neill had claimed that the King had authorised the rising only made the whole situation worse.

To many in England this was the Catholic plot that Pym had been predicting throughout 1641, and perhaps the King had a hand in it. As far as the majority of MPs were concerned, an army had to be raised to save the Protestant position in Ireland and return it to obedience to England. The problem was simple. If such an army was raised, and the King (as was his undoubted constitutional right) was to command it, would this army be used against Catholic rebels or against his then subjects in Parliament? Many MPs did not trust Charles and could not contemplate giving him this power. Charles, on the other hand, took the view that, without control of the armed forces, he had surrendered the most important part of his powers.

There could be no real compromise between these views, and the control of the armed forces was to be the main issue that was to lead to civil war. So events in Ireland determined the course of the next few months and led to the final confrontation of the Nineteen Propositions and the start of the Civil War.

WHY, BY 1642, WAS THERE A CIVIL WAR?

Introduction
In theory, no one in 1640 coming up to what was to be the Long Parliament was thinking of civil war. The majority of MPs were deeply disturbed at the trends, as they saw them, towards absolutism and towards the undermining of the essentially Protestant nature of the Anglican Church. They were well aware that there was a group of Catholics and Catholic sympathisers centred around Henrietta Maria at Court, and Charles's financial and foreign policies in the 1630s had also given cause for concern. As early as the 1620s he seemed to have no real understanding or sympathy for the 'ancient constitution', and the passing of the Petition of Right in 1628 had not really solved that problem. The importance of the Petition of Right in the eyes of many MPs is shown by the references to it in the period 1640–1.

Key themes
- The MPs of November 1640 were strengthened by the undoubted fact that those who elected them seemed to be equally concerned about these trends in the 1630s. The MPs were worried about the possibility of a Roman Catholic conspiracy, but at the same time clear that the 'political nation' was behind them.
- Very few MPs could be seen as real radicals who wished to use the opportunity of Charles's defeat in the Bishops' Wars to force through a programme of forward-looking reform. There were very few identifiable republicans, the most prominent of whom was Henry Marten, and it is significant that his outspoken views were to lead to his imprisonment by Parliament. The country gentlemen going up to Parliament, then, were largely conservatives whose concern was the new directions in which Charles's ministers seemed to be taking him.
- The majority of MPs were moderate Puritans in religion, looking back to the Church of England of James's time, prepared to accept the institution of espiscopacy (bishops), but wanting the moderate bishops

of Elizabeth's and James's time, not the arrogant (as they saw them) 'High Churchmen', such as the Laudian bishops Montagu and Wren. Even those MPs who wished to see the bishops swept away – the Presbyterians such as Denzil Holles – had no intention of taking away the King's prerogatives and removing his power.

Therefore, despite the misgivings of a small minority of MPs over the methods used to destroy Strafford, very few shed any tears for Laud, committed to the Tower in 1641. In general, MPs were not only united but in hope that, with the 'evil counsellors' removed, some sort of agreement with Charles would be possible and that the constitution could be safeguarded. The two key figures that prevented an agreement and a settlement were, of course, Charles himself and John Pym.

The role of Pym

Pym was in some ways the typical Puritan country gentleman. He even had some small 'offices of profit' from the Court in the 1630s while, at the same time, being a member of the Providence Island Company. This was a group of like-minded Puritan country gentlemen who met in those eleven years that Parliament did not sit, in theory to promote formal trading colonies in America, but, as some thought, to organise opposition to Charles's policies. Pym was also a client of the Earl of Bedford – a moderate peer with some Puritan leanings. In every way, then, Pym represented all the main strands of feeling in the House of Commons. This probably accounts for his ability (most of the time) to lead the Commons. Pym was a very clever political operator. For example, when the 'Root and Branch' Petition to abolish bishops and establish Presbyterianism appeared in the House of Commons, firstly as a petition then as a bill, Pym realised that it would totally alienate those moderate Puritan Anglican MPs who opposed Laud but had no wish to see the office of bishop totally abolished. Therefore, he sidelined it, whatever his private feelings might have been.

Pym's belief in a Catholic conspiracy. However, Pym's part in the disaster of 1642 was the result of several factors and his own deeply-held beliefs. Pym really believed in a Roman Catholic conspiracy – however much he played to the gallery over it, it was not a purely political stance. He was well aware of how he was viewed by Henrietta Maria and her circle at Court. He also had the gravest misgivings about Charles's sincerity, whatever his protestation of conventional loyalty in preambles to bills in the House. While Bedford, his patron, lived Pym had not only protection but the possibility of office in an administration that would guide Charles in the 'right direction'.

Pym's position. With Bedford's death in 1641 Pym was on his own. In addition, the death of Bedford made any accommodation between the

Pym group in the Commons and the Court much more unlikely. Without such an accommodation the chances of a settlement between Charles and Parliament were slim. To understand Pym's actions in respect of the crucial autumn and winter session of Parliament, it is important to see that Pym needed the following:

- Firstly, he needed legal protection from royal revenge – so he had to control the machinery of government by forcing himself on Charles as a leading minister.
- Secondly, any dissolution of Parliament (in theory illegal if done by the King after the act for 'a perpetual parliament' – see page 19) would expose him to such revenge. Therefore he had to keep the MPs sitting, believing in a crisis that would prevent them from actually voting for a dissolution themselves.
- Thirdly, he did not trust Charles to rule according to the constitution. With this in mind he had to try to persuade MPs that the King should accept that Parliament should choose the King's ministers and that the King could not be trusted with the armed forces.

Pym's reaction to the Irish Rebellion. Therefore the Irish Rebellion became the first important step on the road to civil war.

- Firstly, it confirmed in Pym's mind, and that of many of his supporters, the thesis that there was a Roman Catholic conspiracy.
- Secondly, it brought into focus an issue that until then was theoretical – command of any armed forces that would have to put down the rebellion.

For Pym, the danger was that Charles, egged on by Henrietta Maria, would use these forces not against the Irish rebels but against his troublesome subjects in Parliament. There had already been two vague 'army plots', and the potential leader of a military coup, Lunsford, had been appointed to the key post of governor of the Tower, so Pym had some reasons for his fears.

The moderates fear Pym. These fears were not shared, of course, by some of the more moderate MPs. Even before the Grand Remonstrance of November 1641, there were signs of unease with Pym's methods, particularly his being prepared to use the London mob to pressurise and intimidate the House of Lords into passing measures. For those 'conservatives' such as Hyde, Falkland and Culpepper, Pym was a dangerous 'rabble rouser'. Their fears about Pym were confirmed when the Grand Remonstrance was printed and published. The Remonstrance itself can be seen as a propaganda document, with its list of the King's actions in the past laid out to justify Pym's 'revolutionary' demands for parliamentary control over appointments to the Council and to the armed forces. No longer could Pym say that he was defending the old constitution. But worse than that for the 'conservatives' was the idea that those who normally took no part in politics would be reading and discussing the Remonstrance. The many-headed monster of public opinion was, once again, being roused by Pym. The passing of the Remonstrance by only eleven votes showed how far control of the Commons had slipped from his hands.

The atmosphere of crisis

The events of 1641–2 cannot be understood unless the background of crisis, fear of plots and riots in which the MPs, the King and the Court had to live, is taken into account. At the time of the debates on Strafford's attainder, rumours of plots to rescue him and a coup by army officers against Parliament were widespread. In one case a sudden sharp cracking noise from the gallery of the House of Commons caused Members to rush out, thinking it was gunfire directed against them. In fact, a fat MP had leant over the gallery and broken some rotten timbers.

Fear of a Roman Catholic conspiracy. The fear of a Roman Catholic conspiracy and uprising was particularly strong after news of the Irish Rebellion had reached England. Richard Baxter, the Presbyterian minister, believed the figure of 200,000 dead that was being bandied about and remarked that when rumours of a plot ran through London the poor people, all the counties over, were ready either to run to arms or hide themselves thinking the papists were ready to rise and cut their throats. Parliament itself listened seriously to several informers who were coming with wild tales of papist risings being organised, or wholesale assassinations of MPs. The reaction to the appointment of Lunsford to command the Tower did not end when Charles withdrew the appointment. Lunsford and some fellow officers got into clashes with citizens around Westminster, clashes that resulted in the death of an MP, Sir Richard Wiseman, and several citizens.

Charles's errors

Many MPs began to see this decay of public order as partly due to Pym's encouragement of **petitioning** and the mob. Deeply conservative men who had a social position to defend could have been swayed at this point had Charles carried on with a policy of reassurance, posing as the natural defender of order and the constitution. Hyde and Falkland had encouraged him to do so, despite the disastrous appointment of Lunsford. He made conciliatory moves, such as entertaining some MPs and giving some knighthoods, but then gave a feast for Lunsford and his fellow officers.

Charles's fundamental mistake was to listen to Henrietta Maria's and Digby's urging of desperate courses. Members who had feared a military coup, and had been told by Pym and his associates that one was imminent, had those fears confirmed. Three hundred troops surrounded the House of Commons, and Charles walked into the chamber – something that the monarch never did. He found the enemies that he wished to arrest, Pym, Strode, Heselrige, Hampden and Holles, already gone, safe in a friendly **City of London** with the one member of the Lords that Charles had marked down – Mandeville.

The effect of the Five Members Coup. The first effect was to rally most of Parliament behind Pym – he was shown to have been right. The King seemed to be in the hands of a desperate group of absolutist-minded advisers with no regard for the law or the constitution. Even Hyde, Falkland and Culpepper were forced to be silent, utterly depressed by the turn of events. Very few spoke in favour of Charles; the only prominent defender he had in Parliament was Sir Ralph Hopton, later to fight for the King.

Charles genuinely believed his life was in danger with the City in such an uproar but his leaving London on 10 January, although understandable, was another error. Once he had left his capital under such circumstances the chance of a settlement between him and Parliament, now sides negotiating at a distance, was much reduced. The war of words between the two sides only poisoned the atmosphere; it did not clear it.

The arming of both sides

The King's immediate moves seemed to be designed to fight a war. Lunsford's attempt to seize an arsenal at Kingston and the King's attempt on the key arsenal at Hull left the impression that negotiation was not really his intention. The Militia Ordinance therefore could be seen as defensive on Parliament's part, while the Commission of Array, the King's attempt to raise forces, was regarded as illegal by many.

Pym's miscalculation

The final step on the road to real war, as opposed to the armed skirmishes that were already taking place as law and order seemed to break down, was the Nineteen Propositions. The Propositions could have taken away nearly all Charles's constitutional rights – the education of his children, control of the armed forces, settlement of the Church, foreign policy, choosing of ministers – which were to be brought under the control of Parliament. Pym's calculation was that, as the Royalist Commission of Array had not succeeded in raising any significant military forces for Charles, he would have to accept these demands, however extreme or, in constitutional terms, 'revolutionary'. For Pym, of course, only these demands could be said to give him and his leading supporters security from any Royalist 'backlash' in the future.

Charles, despite the seemingly hopeless position he found himself in, refused to accept them – probably to Pym's surprise. But when the King formally declared war on 18 August, Pym did not anticipate a long and

---

KEY THEME

Control of the City of London
The Aldermen, rulers of the City, were by no means 'Parliamentarian' in sympathy. They feared disorder more than anything else. Pym's contacts in the city were with the next layer down, the Freemen – smaller merchants, tradesmen, preachers. On 21 December 1641, municipal elections ousted many of the more 'conservative' Aldermen and put control of the City into Pym's hands.

The Parliamentary declaration of 6 September is crucial. It laid down that anyone who did not actively support Parliament would be declared a 'delinquent' and have to pay for any costs of the war. These circumstances forced those 'passive' Royalists who had no enthusiasm for active support to choose sides. They had a traditional loyalty for, but were suspicious of, the King and his Court but had little choice. They chose the King, and at last the King had support.

bloody conflict – the King had few active supporters. Pym made one final miscalculation: the **Parliamentary declaration of 6 September**. Civil war, looming over the horizon for the past six months, had become a reality. This was a war that very few had sought or planned, it was the result of mistrust and miscalculation in an atmosphere of crisis that made all the protagonists unable to calculate coldly or act responsibly.

WHY DID PEOPLE CHOOSE SIDES DURING THE CIVIL WAR?

Introduction

There would have been no war unless the gentry had chosen sides. 'War is a fearful thing', remarked Neville Chamberlain in 1938, and civil war is even more fearful. Many tried to remain neutral and, indeed, probably only 15 per cent of the gentry actively fought on one side or the other. Many of those who supported the war effort, of either Parliament or the King, with money may have wished to stay neutral but had no choice because their area was controlled by either the Royalists or the Parliamentarians. However, enough Englishmen did choose sides to create a war and their motives need to be examined.

Motives for choosing sides

Constitutional issues. For some, constitutional issues were the driving force behind their commitment. For Edmund Ludlow, who eventually became a convinced republican of radical tendencies, 'the Nineteen Propositions were the principle foundation of the ensuing war'.

Equally 'conservatives', such as Hyde, felt that the King's rights were vital to a constitutional balance and that therefore the King not only had right on his side but his enemies were destroying the old foundations of English law and constitution.

Religion. For many, religion was a prime motive. Fear of Roman Catholicism was, as has been noted, one of the strongest forces in English life – a prejudice that ran from the top to the bottom of society. The King's Roman Catholic associates made many deeply suspicious of him and genuinely worried that a royal victory, whatever Hyde's moderate statements said to the contrary, would mean the triumph of Roman Catholicism. Interestingly, although no Catholics fought for Parliament, many of the Roman Catholics wished to remain neutral. On the other side, attacks on the Church of England by many Parliamentarians seemed to mean that the Anglican Church was in danger of being replaced by Presbyterianism or, even worse, by the radical Puritan sects which had sprung into life by 1642. The Laudian bishops had not been loved by many who still supported the Church of England. They were quite happy to see Laud fall – as one Royalist rather heartlessly referred to his captivity in the Tower, 'Canterbury is still afattening' – but the threat posed by Parliament to all bishops, including moderates such as Bishop Hall of Norwich, rang alarm bells and swung many back to the King as the defender of the Church of England.

Of course, Presbyterians, Independents and religious radicals had no reason to support the King and every reason to support Parliament. Only from Parliament could the church reform that they longed for come. Parliament's armies were filled with 'the godly' and, as Oliver Cromwell remarked, 'religion was not the thing at first contested for, but God brought it to that pass in the end'.

Local issues. Local issues could often take precedence over national ones, or at least sway individuals in their allegiances. Leicestershire, for instance, had been used to a long-standing feud between the Grey and Hastings families. A stern Puritan, Lord Grey of Groby of course supported Parliament with dynamism. Inevitably the Hastings supported the King in order to extend the feud, hoping to destroy the Greys. Leicestershire was split down the middle between the supporters of the two families as the Leicestershire gentry had always taken the lead from one or the other. In Suffolk, Sir Nathaniel Barnardiston was a strong Parliamentary supporter – again the lesser gentry were used to following his lead and did so.

Economic interests. Self-interest obviously played a role – the **Monopolists** and **Customs Farmers** supported the Crown, they had no option if they were to have any hope of retrieving their loans. Economic interests could even spill into war contracts; Northampton's support for Parliament was not unconnected with the large boot and shoe contracts given by Parliament. Some of the great territorial aristocracy were Royalist, simply because their own power and status derived from the King and from the institution of kingship: they were all members of the same 'trade union of the great'. Magnates such as the Marquess of Newcastle, who spent over £900,000 on the Royalist cause, and the Marquess of Worcester, who spent over £700,000, saw a Parliamentary victory as a threat to their social and political power. They were to be proved correct. Other aristocrats, of course, did not. Warwick, Essex, Saye and Sele were probably motivated by political and religious principles that put them on Parliament's side, but the majority of the aristocracy supported Charles with varying degrees of enthusiasm.

Traditional loyalties. Traditional loyalties could operate not only on a local level, enabling the leading gentry and aristocrats to get the lesser gentry to follow their lead, but on a national level. This was in the sense that the King was the traditional ruler whom many were accustomed to obey and revere, whatever misgivings individuals may have had about the his conduct, and the idea of rebelling against him was unthinkable. In the last resort, the traditional reverence for monarchy reasserted itself partly because the King was seen by many as 'the keystone that closeth up the arch of Government'. War against the King simply equalled anarchy.

Some Parliamentarians, of course, were also troubled by the concept of war against their sovereign and two lines of thought were produced to reassure them:

- The first, most widely used, was that the King was in the hands of 'evil counsellors' and the war was being fought to free him from them so that Parliament could then come to terms with him without his being led astray by these dark forces.
- The other argument was that the war was not against kingship itself but against a king who had failed to live up to the ideals of kingship.

The parliamentary declaration for 'King and Parliament' showed that for most the idea of actually fighting the King personally was unthinkable. The traditional loyalty to the sovereign sometimes overrode personal inclinations. There may have been many like Sir Edmund Verney, who sympathised with Parliament's aims and had no reverence for bishops, but supported the King (and died for him at Edgehill) because 'my conscience is only concerned . . . to follow my master . . . and [I] will not do so base a thing as to forsake him'.

Mixed motives. The motives for choosing sides for those below the gentry were as mixed. The poor probably made very few decisions – both armies were composed of at least 50 per cent 'pressed men' who, given a choice, would not have been soldiering. The deep-rooted fear of popery on which Parliamentary propaganda played, probably swung many of the small tradesmen, yeoman farmers and artisans – the classes in which Puritan leanings were strong – behind Parliament. Religion was a strong factor amongst the literate classes below the gentry, as Richard Baxter noted.

For many, however, the point about lack of choice held. Stanley, Earl of Derby, simply forced the population in his area to join the Royalist cause, literally threatening to shoot them. Another Royalist in Somerset used economic pressure: 'his tenants most of them holdeth their lands by rack rent, so that if they would not obey his command then out with them'. If lesser gentry were used to following the lead of the greater then this was more pronounced with the 'lower orders'. Both Royalists and Parliamentarians were able to raise forces from their own tenants and retainers in a semi-feudal way.

Conclusion
Any discussion of the motives for choosing sides has to be generalised and incomplete. The Civil War split families, classes and districts and it is

difficult to see one overriding motive for choosing sides. It should be remembered that most went to war reluctantly and without great enthusiasm. Many may simply have chosen the lesser of two evils and Sir Ralph Hopton, the Royalist commander, spoke for many when he wrote to his friend Sir William Waller, the Parliamentary general: 'I detest this war without an enemy.'

WHY DID SO MANY WISH TO REMAIN NEUTRAL IN 1642?

Key themes
- Civil war is far more serious than fighting a foreign enemy. The first few months of the war saw attempts by individuals and counties to remain neutral.
- **John Morrill** has found evidence of attempts at neutrality pacts between many counties. Even counties such as Norfolk, a strongly Parliamentarian one, showed reluctance to engage in conflict. Some of the Norfolk gentry merely voted money for the 'defence of the county'.
- On the county level, raising troops and then not allowing them to leave the county may seem strange. Counties raised troops legally through the Militia Ordinance or, if Royalist-inclined, the Commission of Array, but just because one or other of these legal 'devices' was used does not imply wholehearted support for the side that had framed the legal device.

Loyalty to county. Englishmen still thought of their 'country', i.e. county, as much as if not more than they thought of national interests. Given that the vast majority of the population was not deeply committed to one side or the other, and that most viewed civil war as a disaster, many counties simply raised troops to defend their own county and to keep law and order at a time when it seemed to be dissolving. As the war went on this became a more unrealistic option; counties were dragged into war on a national level and the neutrality pacts between counties, designed to prevent the spread of war, broke down.

Reasons for individuals wishing to remain neutral probably centred around the following:

- Both Pym and Charles had shown themselves uncompromising. Pym's use of the mob had aroused real fear among many of the gentry that the 'lower orders' could take over and so arming them was a very dangerous move. Charles, on the other hand, still appeared to be under the influence not only of the moderate constitutionalist Hyde, but papists and absolutist-minded courtiers. The Five Members Coup, his contacts with the Pope while attempting to raise funds, all left a fear that, given the chance, he would set up an absolutist monarchy. So, for many, both sides seemed to be equally dangerous. Paraphrasing a contemporary: 'If Parliament wins we are invited to perpetual war, if the King should win, a tyranny.'

- Despite support for Parliament among many of the London merchants, merchant communities in provincial towns such as Bristol, Leicester and even Puritan Norwich were fearful of war as it would disrupt trade and raise taxes. Civil war would mean the capture and looting of towns, and the merchants had a lot to lose.

- For many, the terrible example of the Thirty Years War in Germany showed what could happen to a country racked by war. Parts of Germany had become a desert because of a war that had started over religion. A Norfolk petition of January 1643 warned of the 'miserable spectacle of a German devastation'.

- Very few of the gentry had any personal experience of war; they were completely out of their depth as far as fighting was concerned. Some of them had merely obeyed the Militia Ordinance or the Commission of Array in order to defend themselves against increasing social disorder. As Baxter remarked, 'The war was started in our streets before King or Parliament had an army.' Military preparations were seen as a way of actually keeping the lid on an increasingly explosive situation, however unrealistic that might have been.

- If the merchants had much to lose by war, so had the gentry. They could find their lands wasted and their houses burnt, hence the desire expressed by many to keep the war out of their counties.

- War would mean fighting neighbours and former friends or even family members.

- Choosing the wrong side could be fatal. Someone on the losing side could have estates confiscated or be imprisoned, so many of the gentry tried either to delay a decision to commit themselves, a delay made harder after the parliamentary declaration of 6 September, or to give minimum support to one side.

THE CAUSES OF THE CIVIL WAR – HISTORIOGRAPHY

Of all events in English history the Civil War has been the subject of most debate. It has been discussed extensively since the seventeenth century.

Contemporary accounts

Several contemporaries who lived through the events of the 1640s tried to explain them and others wrote their memoirs with comments. The most important contemporary historian is **Edward Hyde, Earl of Clarendon**, who wrote the *History of the Great Rebellion*. He starts his account significantly in 1625, seeing the events of 1625–40 as important in creating a situation where some sort of a breakdown, if not war, was almost inevitable. Clarendon, the great Constitutional Royalist, had been at the centre of events as one of Charles's advisers after the winter of 1642, and an adviser to his son in exile. His history contains somewhat biased portraits of contemporary politicians, and he is critical of Charles's and Laud's policies in the 1630s. But he sees the Civil War as the result of a conspiracy by some self-seeking men, especially Pym, to seize power and destroy the rightful legal position of the King. Clarendon was a conservative, so his dislike of innovations in the 1630s is nothing like his dislike of the events of 1641–2 let alone the subsequent 'revolution' and execution of the King. Whatever his position, his account is the fullest contemporary attempt to chronicle and explain the upheavals.

Edmund Ludlow, a Puritan country gentleman, who was to become a republican and therefore oppose not only monarchy itself but Oliver Cromwell's Protectorate which he saw as a form of monarchy, wrote his memoirs in exile. To Ludlow, the Civil War was a direct result of Charles's attempt, as he saw it, to become an absolutist monarch and Laud's to destroy the Puritan Protestant nature of the Church of England.

After the Restoration of Charles II, historians tended to follow the conservative line of Clarendon, seeing the Civil War as the 'great rebellion', a disastrous event triggered by Pym and his followers.

Whig interpretation

By the nineteenth century attitudes had changed. The political developments of the period, especially the 1832 Reform Act, seemed to show that the pattern of English history was one of gradual change towards more and more freedoms, the result of an inevitable rise in the power of Parliament and a corresponding evaporation in the power of the monarch. Put simply, **Whig** historians, as they were called, said history was about progress and progress could not be stopped. This idea that the central theme of English history was one of onward progress to freedom and democracy became an extremely powerful one, and to a degree has influenced how all English people look at their history. The Whig argument was that the Civil War was a result of an outdated feudal-style monarchy attempting to stop the 'natural' desire of Parliament to have more power.

So, for Whig historians, English history showed that the natural course of history was towards democracy. The nineteenth century saw reform bills extending the vote in 1832, 1867 and 1884. Victorians believed in progress, science, engineering and medicine, so history was also about progress. On that analysis, Charles was preventing 'progress' that was inevitable and natural: the root cause of the breakdown of 1640 and the Civil War itself was the slow, but inevitable, rise of Parliament.

The first great Whig historian was **T B Macaulay** whose *History of England*, written in the 1830s, was one of the most influential works of the nineteenth century, shaping the way English people saw their past. As has already been suggested, Macaulay's view of English history as being progress caught the spirit of the Victorian age.

In the 1880s **S R Gardiner** wrote his monumental history of the early and mid-seventeenth century. Gardiner took great care to use all the possible sources and his research was very thorough. Although later historians have questioned his conclusions, his great achievement has never been surpassed and, to a certain extent, all historians of the period 'stand on his shoulders'. To Gardiner, the Civil War had very long-term causes. As a Whig, the rise of Parliament was one of them. Gardiner called the events of 1640 onwards the Puritan Revolution, seeing Puritanism as not only a religious challenge to the Church of England, but a way of looking at the world which would incline people to be less respectful of traditional authority and more individualistic.

Marxist interpretation

With the rise in influence of Marxism, new interpretations came in the twentieth century. Marx had argued, like the Whigs, that there was a meaning to history, and history was progress. Unlike the Whigs, however, progress did not mean just parliamentary democracy, but eventually a communist state, ruled by the proletariat – the working class. To Marx, economics was the force that changed history. As classes became more economically powerful they overthrew the ruling class and took power themselves. 'All history is the history of the class struggle', wrote Marx. Therefore, in Marxist terms, the feudal system was represented by Charles and it was overthrown by the rising gentry in Parliament – the middle class.

The two leading Marxist-influenced historians are **R H Tawney** and **Christopher Hill**. Hill developed the clearest Marxist interpretation of the whole period 1603–60. For Hill, Puritanism provided the driving force for change because of its emphasis on hard work, and individualism suited the rising gentry who were getting richer as the Crown got poorer. Hill's many distinguished works on the period came close to being an unchallenged interpretation by the early 1960s, even among those who could not, in any way, be called Marxists.

Recent interpretations

In the last 30 years or so, however, there have been two developments in the way the seventeenth century has been viewed. Firstly, there has been an explosion of published work making the period 1603–60 possibly the most written about of all periods in English history. Much of this work modified the Whig and Marxist views.

L Stone argued that it was not so much a 'rise of the gentry', as suggested by Tawney, that upset the balance but a decline in the power and influence of the aristocracy – the King's natural supporters. **Alan Everett** and other 'local' historians argued that our view of the period was distorted by looking at what happened at Court and in Parliament. For most of the gentry, it was local conditions and situations that were important. **Perez Zagorin** argued that the most significant split in society was not an economic/religious one but a cultural one. In his *Court and Country*, he argued that Court culture cut itself off from the lives and attitudes of the country gentry, so creating a gulf which could not be bridged. As more works appeared by historians such as **D Hirst**, **G Alymer**, **C Holmes** and **J Morrill**, the picture painted by the Whig and Marxist historians became increasingly modified, but without an interpretation emerging that seemed to cover the whole period.

In the 1970s a direct attack on the whole basis of the Marxist thesis was made by **Robert Ashton** in his *The English Civil War – Conservatism and Revolution*. Ashton argued that the gentry who formed the anti-Court consensus of 1640 were not politically aggressive, economically self-confident, trying to overthrow a neo-feudal monarchial system, but rather conservatives trying to go back to the 'old constitution' that Charles had undermined. It was Charles who was the 'progressive', the gentry who were the reactionaries – a reversal of the Marxist thesis. Ashton still accepted that there were long-term influences at work in the realm of ideas and that problems existed long before 1640.

Revisionism

However, a more 'extreme' view of the period followed. **Conrad Russell** and, more strongly, **Kevin Sharpe**, took the view that, in fact, nothing went really wrong until 1637 and that there were no long-term causes at all. Historians who took this view were soon labelled **revisionists**. Lately, the revisionists themselves have been subject to revision and there are signs in the work of historians such as **Ronald Hutton** and **Derek Hirst** of a rejection of the more extreme revisionist ideas.

SECTION 2

The Civil War

WHY WAS THERE NO SETTLEMENT AT THE END OF THE FIRST CIVIL WAR?

Introduction

The story of the years 1646–9 is of a three-way search for a solution against a background of potential anarchy, involving the Presbyterian majority in Parliament, the King and a politicised army. None of these three were able to find a viable solution which would satisfy their aspirations.

Key themes

- In the end, it was the army that seized power and, with a small group of their civilian allies, executed the King and set up a Republic. This was a solution that no one had envisaged or considered in 1646. To a great extent, this 'solution' was the result of the incompetence of Denzil Holles and his allies in the Commons and the deviousness of followers of Charles I.
- Indeed, it can be argued that, had Charles immediately made an agreement with Parliament before the radical elements in the army could gain more supporters to come together and act, then a settlement on the lines sought by Pym and the Middle Party in 1643 could have been agreed and accepted.
- It was Charles himself who deliberately set out to play the very dangerous game of dividing his enemies, rather than accepting a settlement which would have allowed him, or his successors, to have regained many of their former powers. Four years of war had made the majority of the English people desperately want peace and certainty, not further upheaval.

The importance of Charles's response. In May 1646 Charles's first move was to surrender, not to his English enemies, but to his other subjects, the Scots. This was probably a first move in dividing his opponents. The Scots, of course, had entered the war to help establish Presbyterianism in England. Typically, Charles was less than frank with them. He seemed to offer the hope of some Presbyterian settlement but his real views were: '[it is] but a temporary permission to continue that unlawful possession (which for the present I cannot help) so as to lay a ground for a perfect recovery of that, which to abandon, were directly against my conscience, and I am confident destructive to monarchy'.

At the same time he received from the Parliament in London the Propositions of Newcastle which laid down that Presbyterianism would be the state church with no other church tolerated. Parliament would control the armed forces for 20 years and his leading supporters should be punished. His reaction was the same as it was to be to all the subsequent offers made to him. He did not make a clear rejection of the Propositions, but in private conversation remarked: 'How to make a handsome denying answer is all the difficulty.'

Parliament, anxious not to negotiate with Charles as a virtual prisoner of the Scots, paid them about half the sum owed to them for their military services and took charge of the King, putting him under easy and honourable house arrest at Holdenby House in Northamptonshire. Holles and the leading Presbyterians saw it as only a matter of time before Charles would agree to their terms, perhaps with some modifications to detail.

Holles's mishandling of the army. However, at the same time, Holles was concerned to disband the army as soon as possible. This was on several grounds:

- it was potentially a dangerous Independent power base;
- the cost could not be born by the enfeebled state – the army was, by this time, living at **free quarter** and the localities were objecting bitterly;
- his own political opponents, both in Parliament and in the army, saw the army as a potential third force to influence the course of events.

In essence, the radical potential of the army was Holles's greatest fear: the moderate men in Parliament wanted to be rid of this threatening monster that they had brought into being. Unfortunately for them, the situation was not de-fused but inflamed by the way the soldiers' quite legitimate demands were treated. The arrears of pay were quite staggering. The infantry were at least eighteen weeks in arrears and the more 'politically aware' cavalry forty-three weeks in arrears. There had already been many mutinies and riots over pay in 1646 amongst various garrisons. The sensible course would have been to make one last effort to pay off the army thus isolating potential troublemakers because probably the majority would have gone home.

- Parliament, however, seemed to go out of its way to inflame the situation.
- Officers who petitioned for pay were threatened with arrest and Holles offered the army as a whole six weeks' pay or service in Ireland.
- At the same time, Holles tried to build up the London militia as a military counter-force to the army, officering it with Presbyterians

under the command of Massey, a very conservative Presbyterian whose loyalties to Parliament in 1643 had even been suspect.

WHY BY 1649 HAD CHARLES BEEN EXECUTED?

Introduction

If Charles had not lost the First Civil War then, of course, his constitutional position, let alone his life and the monarchy itself, would not have been in any danger.

The forces that opposed Charles in 1642 were controlled by the gentry in Parliament, despite their fears of social disorder and the 'lower orders'. Charles was in no personal danger from the vast majority of the MPs in Parliament, nor the gentry officers of the armies of 1642–3. They were fighting to bring the King to terms, to get him to see that he should rule by the constitution as they saw it. Most of them still held to the idea that the King had been led astray by 'evil counsellors' – Digby and Henrietta Maria. If they could be removed then the King would negotiate a settlement.

These Parliamentarians believed they were fighting absolutism and Roman Catholic influences, not their sovereign. Hence Manchester's horror at Cromwell's remark that if he saw the King in battle he would shoot at him. At this stage, however, even the likes of Cromwell were seeing the future in terms of a settlement after a Parliamentary victory.

The rise of the radicals

By 1646, however, the conservative gentry who had gone to war to preserve the constitution were faced with a challenge from their own supporters. The New Model army, created to win the war, was itself becoming politicised and radical. Leveller ideas had spread and some of the troops were beginning to demand the right to take part in any settlement. The seed for this attitude had been sown by the spread of religious radicalism under the influence of unauthorised preaching and even some radical army chaplains such as Hugh Peter. Given that any settlement under the Solemn League and Covenant of 1643 would be a Presbyterian one, the growing influence of Independency was pointing to a potential split between Parliament and its army. Soldiers and officers, such as Cromwell, wanted religious toleration to be part of any settlement; the Presbyterian majority in Parliament did not. Some of the Independents in the army became not only religiously radical but politically radical too.

The attitude of the Levellers. For Levellers, such as Sexby, speaking at the Putney Debates in the autumn of 1647, the soldiers had fought and won a war and were entitled to a say in any settlement: 'There are many thousands of us soldiers that have ventured our lives to recover our birthrights and privileges as Englishmen.' Rainborough's appeal was clear: 'For I really think that the poorest he that is in England hath a life to live as the greatest he . . . I think it is clear that every man that is to live under a government ought first, by his own consent, to put himself under that government.' This was summed up by Wildman: 'I conceive that's the undeniable maxim of government: that all government is in the free consent of the people.'

Although senior officers such as Cromwell and Ireton were alarmed by some of these truly revolutionary ideas, their alarm was as nothing compared with the panic of the gentry in Parliament. A 'party' had arisen that had no voice in 1642 and was to all intents and purposes republican and radical. The Leveller Petty, although prepared to see a settlement that protected property, had no brief for monarchy: 'I hope that they may live to see the power of the King and the Lords thrown down.'

The 'conservative' Parliamentarians' mistake

The situation that led to the Putney Debates would probably not have happened but for the desire of Holles and his supporters in Parliament to disband the army as rapidly as possible, while at the same time not paying the army the large arrears of pay that were due to them.

Holles and the Presbyterian MPs mishandled the situation, playing into the hands of the radicals and uniting the army in their suspicion and dislike of their former masters. They voted only six weeks' pay, declared that the army should be only 6000 strong and that only Presbyterians should be officers. The most influential officers were Independents, the army were eighteen weeks in arrears of pay for the foot (infantry) and up to forty-three weeks for the horse (cavalry). By the end of May 1647 the then Parliament had thoroughly alienated the army. The Army Rendezvous of June (when the army were called together at Newcastle to discuss grievances), the Heads of Proposals, the Putney Debates all followed.

Holles's fears of 'beggars riding on horses' was the voice of the conservative gentry MPs, and it had come to pass, but largely because he had united the army rather than placating them by making a fair offer. If Holles and the Presbyterians had treated the army fairly in the spring of 1647, then it is perfectly possible that the radical Levellers and even the more conservative Independent officers would have been isolated, as the army accepted their pay and went home. As it was, Holles created the very monster he feared – an Independent, politically-radicalised army that would challenge Parliament for the right to negotiate a settlement. The gentry in Parliament who had gone to war in 1642 for the constitution now found themselves side-lined by an army that could enforce settlement.

Charles's miscalculations

Charles, from the moment he surrendered to the Scots in May 1646, totally miscalculated the rapidly changing situation. In all his negotiations with Parliament and the army he held to the following ideas:

- Firstly, any concessions he gave were temporary, to gain time and were not genuine.
- Secondly, all his opponents, Scots, Presbyterians, Independents, soldiers and Parliamentarians, were traitors against their anointed sovereign, so any concession he agreed to could be withdrawn. It was no sin to mislead traitors who were damned anyway as they had rebelled against God's representative on earth. He utterly failed to see that any of his opponents could also have principles.
- Thirdly, he failed to distinguish between his opponents in terms of the danger they might represent to him, and their ability to enforce any settlement reached. The fact that Holles and his allies in Parliament were not in a position to enforce a settlement if the army did not accept it does not seem to have occurred to him. Nor does the threat posed by radical republicanism in the army itself.
- Fourthly, his ploy was to prolong negotiations as long as possible in the hope that the forces that defeated him – the Parliament, the army, the Presbyterians and the Independents – could 'fall out amongst themselves', as Sir Jacob Astley had predicted in 1646 when he surrendered the last Royalist army to Parliamentary forces. Charles saw himself as crucial to any settlement, and if his opponents were to fall out then he would be the arbitrator between them. He simply could not conceive of a settlement without him.

The significance of the Second Civil War, 1648

What sealed Charles's fate was the Second Civil War in the spring of 1648. Parliament, with the Vote of No Addresses, broke off negotiations but the army went further in its outrage. At the Windsor Prayer Meeting, Colonel Goffe, a religious enthusiast and ally of Cromwell, expressed the united feeling of the army that it was: 'Our duty, if ever the Lord brought us back to peace, to call Charles Stuart, that man of blood to an account for the blood he had shed, and mischief he had done, against the Lord's cause and the people in these poor nations'. The conservative Presbyterian majority in the House of Commons, once the war was over, attempted to reopen negotiations with Charles but they were negotiating with a corpse.

Some of the Independents and indeed Presbyterians in Parliament had decided that Charles was never prepared to negotiate, but the army even more so. Ireton, not Cromwell, was the driving force behind Pride's

Purge in December 1648. The conservative Presbyterians were powerless to continue negotiations with the King at Newport – the army held the real power in the land, determined and united to try the King. Cromwell seems to have wavered on his return to London, but once he had made up his mind he supported the trial wholeheartedly.

Therefore, the execution of Charles was the result of the following:

- his never accepting the verdict of the First Civil War;
- his belief that there could be no settlement without him;
- the impotence of those such as Holles who wanted a settlement with him.

Many of those who had decided on execution, civilians and soldiers such as Ireton and Cromwell, were not true 'radical republicans' – they had come to believe that there could be no peace while Charles lived. Ironically, he was not a symbol of order but the cause of constant war and disorder. Gradually the realisation of Charles's attitude dawned on some who were negotiating with him – not the 'conservative' Parliamentarians but the army officers and their Independent allies in Parliament.

Therefore, instead of being the key figure representing order in any settlement, Charles had come to be viewed as the key figure in continuing disorder. Also his failure to see the threat of a politicised army was crucial. Even at his execution he never saw that new principles, deeply-held, could be real. When soldiers called for 'Justice! Justice! Execution!', he remarked: 'Poor soldiers. For a piece of money, they would do the same for their Commanders.'

The power of the minority. Those who decided, and carried out, the execution of Charles I were a small minority of the political nation that had gone to war in 1642. Nevertheless, they were a minority with the power to cut the stranglehold of war and fruitless negotiations that were the hallmarks of 1646–9. Charles had failed to see the power of this minority. It may be that there were many others who, although flinching from the decision to execute an anointed sovereign, may have seen it as Cromwell is reputed to have done, as a 'cruel necessity'. In the last resort Charles I was executed, not because he was king, but because he was Charles I: stubborn, devious and uncomprehending.

Many of those who 'accepted' regicide after the event were by no means convinced republicans but Charles had left them no choice.

ASSESSMENT: THE CIVIL WAR

ESSAY QUESTIONS IN THE STYLE OF OCR (AS)

Introduction. You will be expected to do the following:

- Analyse throughout the essay. This can be done by making sure that you plan a line or argument before you start writing. At the start of each paragraph you must make the next point of your argument, explain it and then use evidence to back your point up (see next point). There is a clear difference between narrative (telling the story) and analysis (putting forward a reasoned argument in response to a question). A tip for how to ensure that you are *analysing*. You need to start each paragraph with words which will lead onto analysis. These might include:
The most important reason.........
Another key point is that............
One should argue that...............
Essentially.............
If you use the following words at the start of a paragraph you are more likely to fall into a narrative style of writing:
In (followed by a date)........
This was followed by ....
- Back up your argument by using well selected evidence. The evidence you select must be accurate and relevant to the point you are trying to make.
- Make a clear and consistent attempt to reach a judgement. In your essay you must argue throughout. You must reflect on the evidence you have given and make points which answer the question directly.
- Show evidence of independent thought. You do not have to be original. Independent thought means that you have reflected on what you have read in this and other books and that you can explain the ideas that you have picked up in your own words.
- Language skills. It is essential that you write in paragraphs, that you are grammatically accurate.

Here are two tips to help you write well:

- Always read your work through after you have finished and correct any errors.
- Get into the habit of structuring your essays in such a way that a new point of your argument means a new paragraph.

Personal Rule and Civil War, 1629–49

Reading

The question below is very wide ranging in its scope. Before answering this question you should have read Chapters 1–3.

> 1 From November 1640 to the outbreak of Civil War in August 1642, the Long Parliament was involved in a series of disputes with the King. These areas of dispute included:
> * the financial affairs of the Crown
> * control of the armed forces
> * the religion of the nation
> * the King's ministers.
>
> a) Explain why any two of these disputes led to division between King and Parliament. (30)

How to answer this question

To answer this question, and questions of a similar style, you need to do the following:

* Focus on the concept of 'division'. There are obvious links between all four factors given; however you must focus on the link between the factors you have chosen and a clear explanation of why they led to division.
* You are being asked to show a high degree of understanding. Therefore you will need to analyse the importance of your two chosen factors. You must not simply describe the factors or tell a story of events.

Plan

In your plan you should try to refine your argument by showing how the factors you have chosen led to division. It might be worth pointing out that these divisions did not automatically lead to civil war.

Here are examples of points you could make in your introduction and then expand upon throughout your answer.

* The issue of the religion of the nation was crucial to division between Parliament and King.
* Suspicion of popery at Court and the influence of Laud led to a wider mistrust of the King's intentions.
* Religion and politics were linked in the belief in a Roman Catholic/absolutist conspiracy.

- Control of the armed forces was linked to mistrust of the King. During and after the Irish Rebellion in 1641 there were many in Parliament who feared that Charles would use control of the army to reassert Personal Rule.

Style
Below is an example of the style you might write in. Please note that the style is direct and attempts to link clearly the factors to division.

The Irish Rebellion is, perhaps, the single most important factor that led to division in the autumn of 1641. It brought the issue of control of the armed forces and fear of a military takeover by Charles to a head. The situation in 1641 created a crisis because the question of command of the armed forces was no longer a theoretical one, but a pressing practical one.

Pym constantly demanded that Parliament have some say in the control of the armed forces. Neither Pym nor the King could give way on this because it went to the heart of the debate about the extent of the King's powers. Because of the Irish revolt an army would have to be raised to put down the rebellion and the King had the undoubted right to command the army. However, Pym and many in Parliament feared that he would use it against them.

Division came from the fact that at this point the King listened to the 'absolutist' clique at Court led by Henrietta Maria. Thomas Lunsford, popularly supposed to be the sort of adventurer who would involve himself in a military coup, was appointed as governor of the Tower of London. It seemed to be a confirmation of Charles's secret desire to regain freedom of action through a military coup. Under pressure, Charles then cancelled the appointment. Had Charles appointed the Earl of Essex as commander of the troops to be raised for the reconquest of Ireland, he would have made a military appointment which would have reassured the House of Commons. Essex was associated with all the 'reforms' of the past year. Division again was increased by the failure of Charles to nominate any commander.

> **b)** Compare the importance of at least three of these disputes in causing the outbreak of Civil War in 1642. (60)

How to answer this question
The key to answering this type of question is to compare the difference in importance of the factors. To gain the top level you must do the following:

- You should plan an argument before you start and then follow that argument throughout your answer.
- You must provide enough evidence to back up your answer.

- Try to link the factors together. Where you can, try and evaluate the relative importance of the factors.

Plan

You should try to identify the main points of your argument which will help you answer the question. You should also include a list of what you are going to write about in each paragraph.

- A background reason for division was mistrust which came from the different cultures of Court and Parliament.
- This difference was in part due to differences in religion. The view of Charles as a papist sympathiser put him at odds with many of Parliament's leaders.
- Linked to fear of Charles using force to impose absolutist rule was the issue of control of the armed forces.
- The financial policies of Personal Rule had created anxiety among the Parliamentary gentry.

ESSAY QUESTION IN THE STYLE OF AQA (A2)

General points. To answer this type of essay question you need to do the following:

- Read the question carefully and identify what the question is asking you.
- The response to the question needs to be direct and to the point.
- Before you start to write you should plan your answer carefully. In your plan you should include a list of points which will form the basis of your argument/judgement. You should then briefly map out what you plan to put in each paragraph.
- Start your answer with a brief introduction. Choose evidence to back up the points you have made and use it in your answers.
- Conclude in such a way that you clearly state the judgement you have made in response to the question.

Read Source A and then answer the question that follows.

Source A

The English Civil War was not an isolated event. Charles ruled over three kingdoms, and within three years he faced armed resistance in all three of them, Scotland in 1639, Ireland in 1641, and England in 1642.

Conrad Russell, *The Causes of the English Civil War*, 1990.

1 How important were events in Scotland and Ireland in contributing to the eventual outbreak of civil war in England in 1642? (20)

How to answer this question

This is a type of question which demands an 'up to a point . . . but' response. This question asks you to explain the Civil War in the wider context of events in Ireland and Scotland. It is asking you to base part of your response on an analysis of the factors which are common to England, Scotland and Ireland. These include:

- The problems Charles had in raising an army to tackle the crises in Ireland and Scotland.
- The issue of religious differences and tension in and between Ireland, England and Scotland.
- Charles's attempts to centralise.

Although these points were important, they need to be understood in the context of other factors such as the mistakes made by Charles in his dealings with Parliament. Long-term financial and religious issues were essential.

Plan

Your argument in your plan might include points such as these:

The issues in Scotland and Ireland were important in that they highlighted the issue of religious differences and increased mistrust of Charles.

However, these factors in themselves did not make war inevitable. They acted as a catalyst for other deep-rooted problems including the issue of the nature of Charles's kingship and his intentions with regards to religion.

Style

Below is an extract from an answer to this question. It is from a paragraph about the impact of the Irish Rebellion. Note how the candidate attempts to answer the question directly.

The importance of the Irish Rebellion is that it created the final crisis that was to transform a situation of mutual suspicion and distrust into a crisis the effects of which were to propel England into civil war. The effect of the news of the 1641 rebellion (or massacre as it was called at the time) cannot be over estimated. To many in England this was the Catholic plot that Pym had been saying, throughout 1641, was brewing, and perhaps the King had a hand in it. As far as the majority of MPs were concerned, an army had to be raised to save the Protestant position in Ireland and return it to obedience to England. The problem was simple. If such an army was raised, and the King (as was his undoubted constitutional right) was to command it, would this army be used against Catholic rebels or against his then subjects in Parliament? Many MPs did not trust Charles and could not contemplate giving him this power. Charles, on the other hand, took the view that, without control of the armed forces, he had surrendered the most important part of his powers. There could be no real compromise between these views and the control of the armed forces was to be the main issue that was to lead to civil war. So events in Ireland determined the course of the next few months and led to the final confrontation of the Nineteen Propositions and the start of the civil war.

SOURCES QUESTIONS IN THE STYLE OF EDEXCEL/OCR (AS)

The world turned upside down: Monarchy and Republic in England, 1646–53

Reading

Before answering the questions you should read Chapter 5 (pages 50–61) in this book.

Study Sources A to E and then answer questions 1 to 5.

Source A

(*The title page of a pamphlet published in 1647.*)

Source B
(From a letter from Cromwell to his cousin Colonel Robert Hammond, 25 November 1648. Cromwell is giving his views about the Treaty of Newport.)

Do you not think this fear of the Levellers (of whom there is no fear) that they would destroy nobility, had caused some to make this ruining hypocritical agreement. Has this fear influenced even some good men? Has this fear caused some of our friends to think that people may have as much good one way as the other. That is, that they may have just as much good by this man [Charles I] against whom the Lord hath witnessed.

Source C
(John Lilburne was a leading Leveller. This is his account of Cromwell's speech to the Council of State which was made after he was taken from the room, but which he overheard. Lilburne was brought before the Council of State in March 1649.)

"I tell you sirs," Cromwell declared, thumping the table, "You have no other way to deal with these men but to break them or they will break you and bring all the guilt of the blood and treasure shed and spent in this Kingdom upon your heads and shoulders and frustrate and make void [destroy] all the work that, with so many years' industry, toil and pains you have done . . . Sirs, I tell you again, you are necessitated to break them."

Source D
(From Cromwell's speeches at the Putney Debates, October 1647. He is discussing the proposals in the Agreement of the People.)

Truly this paper does contain in it very great alterations to the government of the kingdom. And what would that produce but an absolute desolation – an absolute desolation to the nation? We must consider whether what is proposed can be done; that is to say whether the people of this nation are prepared to go along with it.

There will be very great mountains in the way of this and, therefore, we ought to consider the consequences. It is not enough to propose things that are good in their aims . . . I say it to you again, I shall offer nothing to you but that I think in my heart and conscience tends to the uniting of us.

Source E
(Ware was the defeat of the Leveller mutiny in the army in November 1647.)

Ware was a defeat for the Levellers from which they had little hope of recovery. Their one hope of even temporary success was to win the support of the army:

the attempt had failed, the Council of the Army was soon dispersed, and no such opportunity ever presented itself again. Outside the army they had many supporters, especially in and around London, but not amongst the classes which traditionally held political power. Only in the army was there a possible alternative power base through which a fundamental change might have been brought about.

A L Morton, *Freedom in Arms*, 1974.

1 Study Source A. What evidence is there to show that the author of the pamphlet disapproved of the radical ideas circulating at the time? (3)

How to answer this question

The question is asking you to show that you understand the source. Therefore you must:

- Provide some explanation which answers the question.
- Refer to the source to back up what you are saying.

Style

Here is an example of the style you should use:

The source contains the words 'ridiculous' and 'distracted', whilst the title is 'The World Turned Upside Down'. This indicates disapproval. The pictures show the normal world reversed. The author writes that he is a well-wisher to the King, Parliament and Kingdom. The mention of the King also indicates he would not approve of radical ideas.

2 Use your own knowledge to explain how the Levellers in the army were influential in October 1647. (5)

How to answer this question

The question is asking you to explain the influence of the Levellers in the army in 1647. Therefore you need to respond with a thorough explanation which takes in at least some of the following points:

- You should show how and why the Levellers in the army were influential as a radical group with a power base in 1647.
- You should show why by 1647 radical ideas had become more acceptable and how the Levellers challenged Ireton and Cromwell over the nature of government.
- You should show why events had put the army in a strong political position by 1647.

3 Study Sources B and C and refer to both sources in your answer. Explain how accurately you think Lilburne has reported Cromwell's views. (6)

How to answer this question

You need to look for examples of accuracy in the sources. The question asks you to use the sources and you need to focus on what they say in your answer.

Plan

Before you write you need to come to some kind of conclusion about how you will answer the question. An example might be as follows:

This statement is not convincing. Lilburne's account is unreliable given his opposition to Cromwell. However, the nature and origin of Source B showing Cromwell's attitude to fear of the Levellers meant that his views have to be treated with caution.

However, doubts about Lilburne's motives as shown in Source C should also be addressed.

Style

Make sure that you quote from the sources when making your point. Below is an example of a suitable style:

Although Source B differs in tone and content from the message of Source C, this may well not be because of Lilburne's inaccuracy. Cromwell is using the alleged threat of the Levellers which he does not share to try to attack those in favour of the Treaty of Newport, "this ruining hypocritical agreement".

4 Study Sources B and D. Compare the value of Sources B and D as evidence to the historian studying Cromwell's attitude to the Levellers. (5)

How to answer this question

When answering a question about the value of a source you should try to avoid generalisations about the type of source and you should concentrate on more than its content. Instead you should ask yourself the following questions:

- What is the situation of the author of the source?
- Is the author in a position to know about the subject of the source?
- In your view has the author used the full range of sources available at the time? Has the author dealt with the different views from the time? How has the author dealt with gaps in his/her evidence? Has he/she simply ignored them?
- What is the purpose of the author in producing the source?
- Has the author deliberately distorted the evidence?
- Is the source produced as propaganda?
- What are the limitations of each source as well as their positive points?

Style

Try to refer to the sources whenever possible to back up your ideas. To gain top marks you need to ensure that you cover both sources. Below is an example of the style you might choose to use.

> Cromwell's views about the Levellers were complicated. This is shown by the sources. On the one hand he sympathised to an extent with their proposals, in Source D he speaks of the Levellers being 'good in their aims'. The value of this evidence is that it shows that, at the Putney Debates, Cromwell hoped to be conciliatory. However, it is also valuable in showing us that Cromwell's views of the Levellers were tainted by the view that he saw them as potentially divisive.

5 Using Sources B, C and E and your own knowledge explain why the Levellers' proposals had little chance of success. (12)

How to answer this question

This question asks you to analyse the reasons why the Levellers' ideas had little chance of being put into effect. To reach full marks you will need to do the following:

- Look for a variety of reasons to explain why the Levellers' proposals had little chance.
- Prioritise your most important reasons.
- Use information from both the sources and your own knowledge.
- Plan your line of argument first and then what you are going to put in each paragraph.

Plan

You might use these points of argument in your plan:

- The majority of the army trusted Cromwell, rather than the Leveller spokesmen.
- The majority was more interested in bread and butter issues such as pay and indemnity rather than paper constitutions.
- The Levellers, as already noted, had no clear leadership or organisational structure. Their most dynamic army representative, Colonel Rainborough, was killed in the Second Civil War.
- Cromwell put down the Leveller mutinies at Corkbush (1647) and Burford (1649) very rapidly before they could get out of hand, which showed their weakness.

PART 2: THE ENGLISH REPUBLIC, 1649–60

INTRODUCTION

The English Republic
After the execution of Charles I, the Rump Parliament and Council of State ruled a divided, confused country. The Rump faced many problems at home and abroad and did not succeed in persuading the majority of the nation wholeheartedly to support it.

By 1653 disillusionment with the Rump was widespread. It was seen as a narrow group of MPs who, on the one hand, had agreed to, or accepted, the execution of the King but, on the other hand, had not brought in reforms that some wished for. The army, in particular, was disillusioned with the Rump and in the spring of 1653, led by the Commander-in-Chief Oliver Cromwell, the army overthrew it. The Rump was replaced by a 'nominated assembly'; not elected by anyone but chosen by the army.

By the winter of 1653 this assembly, dominated by religious fanatics, had also lost credibility and it was replaced by the Protectorate of Oliver Cromwell. Cromwell tried to balance all the differing forces and groups that had appeared as a result of the upheavals of the 1640s, but failed to create a lasting settlement. His two Parliaments could not be called successes but he did provide some stability in this difficult period, and it is possible that, had he lived longer, the country would have settled down under the Lord Protector.

He had refused the Crown in 1657 when a group in Parliament offered it to him, but he was moving towards a more settled 'conservative' regime when he died in September 1658. The theme of the years 1649–58 is that of a 'quest for settlement' after the upheavals of the 1640s,

and there is still debate over Cromwell's successes and
failures in this quest.

AS: NARRATIVE AND EXPLANATION

CHAPTER 7

The Rump and Barebones Parliaments, 1649–53

BACKGROUND TO THE RUMP PARLIAMENT

Introduction
There are different names given to the governments of this period.

- The whole period, 1649–60, is known as the Interregnum – a period without a monarch.
- The Commonwealth refers to the period January 1649 to December 1653 and again from April 1659 to March 1660 when a republican 'Rump' Parliament sat.
- The period December 1653 to April 1659 is known as the Protectorate, firstly Oliver Cromwell's, and then, after Oliver's death in September 1658, his son Richard's – until his fall in April 1659 when the Rump was restored.

Thus the entire period is known as the Commonwealth and Protectorate, the English Republic, the British Republic (as Scotland and Ireland were later joined to England and returned Members of Parliament to Westminster) or the Interregnum.

The Rump, 1649–53
The **Rump Parliament** had to deal with many problems:

- External problems – rebellion in Ireland, Scottish/ Royalist invasion and, later, war with the Dutch.
- It also had economic problems. 1649 and 1650 were marked by bad harvests causing considerable social distress. The regime also had a mountain of debt.

KEY TERM

The Rump Parliament The Rump was the name given to the Parliament that sat after the execution of Charles, at first consisting only of MPs who had agreed to the trial of the King. 'Rump' meant a small part that was left. The name was first used insultingly by the Presbyterian MP excluded by Pride's Purge, Clement Walker, who referred to 'this Rump of a Parliament with corrupt maggots in it'.

- Politically it faced potential opposition from both conservatives and radicals.
- Many were simply not prepared to accept a government associated with the ultimate crime (as they saw it) of regicide (the murder of the King).
- The Rump needed the support of the army, but the army always wanted to push it in the direction of reforms in the law and in other political areas which would have made it even more unacceptable to the conservative gentry, both Royalist and Presbyterian, who had supported Parliament.
- The MPs who sat in the Rump were themselves, in the main, fairly conservative. They had reluctantly agreed to the execution of the King, or accepted it afterwards, only because they could see no other course of action that would bring peace, not because they were convinced republicans. For them the 'revolution' ended in 1649 – it was not the first stage towards some real changes in the politics of England.
- Even MPs, such as **Sir Arthur Heselrige**, Thomas Scot and Sir Henry Vane, who were convinced republicans, were not in any other way in favour of sweeping political or social changes. To have set up a Republic was enough.

Therefore, the Rump continually 'fell between two stools'; not radical enough for those who expected sweeping political or religious changes, not 'respectable' enough to attract the wholehearted support of a large section of the gentry.

The Republic established, 1649. With the execution of the King, slowly the Rump moved towards setting up a Republic. The House of Lords was abolished on 6 February 1649, on 7 February the monarchy was formally abolished and on 14 February the Council of State, the executive or governing body of the Republic, was set up.

The return of some members. Significantly, over 100 MPs, who had absented themselves at the time of Pride's Purge, were readmitted during February and these were, naturally, of a more conservative mind. Many others (the excluded members) of course refused even to contemplate trying to get back in, seeing Pride's Purge as a totally illegal act.

The Great Seal of the Commonwealth.

Sir Arthur Heselrige was a strong Puritan, first coming to prominence opposing Laud and Strafford, and one of the Five Members marked down by Charles in January 1642. Heselrige raised his own regiment during the First Civil War. Prominent in the Rump Council of State, he consistently opposed Cromwell after 1652 and was seen as the leader of the republican 'Commonwealth's-men'. He played a leading part in the downfall of Richard Cromwell and avoided execution when Charles II returned. He died in prison in 1661.

Sir Arthur Heselrige.

The engagement. In January 1650 the Rump then succeeded in alienating the traditional elements in the political nation who might have been prepared to accept and cooperate with them despite the fact that they had killed the King. They cut themselves off from potential support by imposing an 'engagement', requiring all adult males to 'engage obedience' to the current Parliament. The main features of the engagement were as follows:

- it was ordered to be taken by all;
- those who took it promised obedience to 'the Commonwealth as is now established without a King or House of Lords';
- refusal to take the engagement meant being barred from all public offices;

- in practice it meant acceptance that Pride's Purge and the execution of the King were legal.

This was too much for many former Parliamentarian and Royalist gentry who simply dropped out of public life. They might have been prepared to serve the Rump on the basis that at least it was a government and therefore better than anarchy or rule by the **radicals**, or the army. But to accept the legality of the events of 1648–9 was unthinkable. So, from the beginning, the Rump's base of support was narrow.

Religious toleration. The Rump also did little to reassure the religious radicals and Independents on the question of religious toleration when they introduced a series of **religious acts**.

- The act enforcing attendance at church was only repealed by the casting vote of the Speaker, such was the strength of the conservative Presbyterians, most of whom had returned after Pride's Purge.
- Frightened of the sects, the Rump passed a blasphemy act in August 1650. Also, an act was passed in May making adultery a capital offence.

Religious radicalism in the 1650s. There had been very radical religious ideas coming to the surface but with the execution of the King religious radicalism increased. There were also radical political groups which emerged, including the **Diggers**. Some of the radicals saw the execution as a sign of the coming of Christ – the last days. There were several sects who gained some support in this period.

- The **Ranters** claimed that nothing was a sin unless you believed you had sinned. They were opposed by most other religious groups.
- The **Fifth Monarchists** were the most important. They had supporters in the army in London and Wales. Fifth Monarchists believed that the end of the world was coming, and Christ would return. Their ideas were interpretations of the books of Daniel and Revelation in the Bible. The prophecy in Daniel refers to four great monarchies falling – the fifth monarchy would last forever. Therefore, believed the Fifth Monarchists, this

KEY THEME

Attitude of the radicals to the Rump From the beginning, some radicals viewed the Rump with suspicion. Lilburne, imprisoned by the Council of State, produced his pamphlet, *Englands New Chains Discovered*. The title said all that the Levellers thought of the Rump.

KEY THEME

Effects of the religious acts The acts do not seem to have been very effectively carried out. Only four people were executed for adultery, while even the most radical sects (small groups of religious radicals) continued to operate, despite being persecuted.

KEY TERM

The Diggers The Diggers or 'True Levellers' were the most radical political group. Their leader, Gerard Winstanley, was a remarkable political thinker in his radicalism. He believed that all property should be held in common, all land belonged to everybody: 'The earth was a common treasury.' He set up a 'commune' at St George's Hill in Surrey in 1650. The Rump Council of State was concerned, but the army officers it sent down to investigate found the Diggers harmless eccentrics. However, they were moved on. Winstanley tried to start another commune on common land at Wellingborough in Northamptonshire in 1651. He seems to have had some sympathy and help from local people, but the Council of State instructed the local JPs to break it up. After that Winstanley lost heart.

monarchy would be the reign of King Jesus. The previous monarchies had been Babylon, Persia, Greece and Rome. The execution of King Charles, whom they believed was a Roman Catholic, signalled the end of the fourth monarchy. Their leader was John Rogers and their ally in the army was Major General Harrison. After 1653 they lost influence but even in 1661 the Fifth Monarchist Venner, with a handful of followers, was able to attempt an armed uprising in London, which was easily put down.

- The **Quakers**, the most important of the later sects, spread from the preaching of George Fox, although they had no formal organisation and many religious radicals could claim to be Quakers that did not share all their beliefs. Quakers relied entirely on the 'inner light' – personal religious experience – and rejected all forms of church organisation and discipline. They also seemed to be subversive of social order, refusing to take off their hats in respect for judges, officers and gentry. At first they interrupted church services. The Quakers were the largest of the sects.

IRELAND AND SCOTLAND AND THE DOWNFALL OF THE RUMP

Ireland

External threats were the first priority of the Rump. Ireland had not been reconquered since the rebellion of 1641. Irish Royalists were holding out, in real terms, in an uneasy alliance with the Roman Catholics. They disliked each other, but hated the Republic more. The 'threat' from Ireland was not, as will be seen, as dangerous as that from Scotland, but the reconquest of Ireland was a necessity for the Rump for the following reasons:

- It would keep a potentially restless army occupied.
- The massacres of 1641 should be avenged and the 'Protestant acendency' confirmed.
- Royalism still held out in Ireland and it was feared that Ireland, as so many times in the past, could be used as a potential 'backdoor' springboard for an invasion of England – in this case, by Charles Stuart, the eldest son of Charles I.

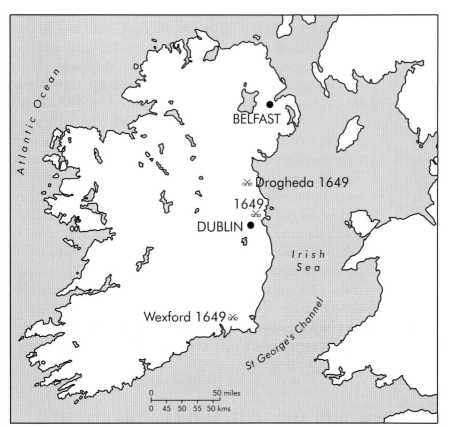

Cromwell's campaigns. Cromwell landed in Ireland in August 1649, determined to strike rapidly at the Earl of Ormonde, the Royalist leader, before winter set in. The key garrison towns of Drogheda and Wexford were stormed by October, with the garrisons slaughtered. Early in the following year Cromwell left Ireland, having smashed any armies that might have resisted. The rest of the Irish campaign, with its guerrilla warfare, went on with Ireton commanding the English forces. The divisions among the Irish themselves – confederate Catholics refusing to cooperate with Royalists – also helped towards the final defeat of 1652, by which time Ireton himself had died of malaria.

Significance of the Irish campaign. Other factors also played a part in the Irish campaign. Cromwell was very anxious to win the 'old' Anglo-Irish gentry from their allegiance to the Royalist cause, and his success with Lord Broghill was a key factor in bringing over many of them to

Cromwell's campaign in Ireland.

the Republic's side. Also, Michael Jones, Governor of Dublin, had already defeated Ormonde at Rathmines before Cromwell arrived in Ireland. Cromwell's success in Ireland made him an even more important figure in English affairs, as well as being the symbol, for the Roman Catholic Irish, of English oppression.

Scotland

Scarcely had the Irish campaign begun to die down than a greater threat to the Republic became clear. In February 1649 the Scots had proclaimed Charles II as King. At first, this was not much more than a gesture because practical Scottish help for Charles to regain his throne in England, and for him to be crowned King of Scotland, depended on his being prepared to abandon Anglicanism and take the Presbyterian covenant. Charles, in Holland, prolonged his discussions with the Scots in the hope that either the Royalist Montrose, still fighting in Scotland, or Ormonde in Ireland would have decisive victories which could give him an independent Royalist power base.

Cromwell in Ireland put paid to Ormonde, while Montrose was defeated and executed by the Presbyterians, whose religious convictions overrode support for Charles II. Now Charles had no choice: he had to accept the terms of the Scottish Presbyterians whom he hated. He even had to make a public statement opposing his father's and mother's religion.

Dunbar, 1650. Cromwell led an army across the border in June 1650, winning a victory at Dunbar in September. His army of 3000, hemmed in by the sea on one side and therefore in theory at a tactical disadvantage, defeated a Scottish army of 10,000. He then set about reducing the rest of Scotland, helped by the divisions among the Scots, many of whom had only reluctantly taken up Charles's cause.

The 'Third' Civil War

Charles Stuart invaded England in the summer of 1651 at the head of another Scottish army, but the English Royalists, who disliked his Scottish allies and hated the prospect of another civil war, did not rise to support him.

The Dunbar Medal.

Charles II.

At the Battle of Worcester, on 3 September 1651, Cromwell defeated Charles with the New Model army and the help of the local militia troops. This was a significant comment on the popularity of Royalism. After Worcester, Charles fled abroad and the Republic never faced a serious military threat again.

Charles's lucky escape, and the bravery of those who sheltered him, has become a legend. However, this legend should not obscure the fact that, for the majority of the country, Charles's invasion was a potential disaster and he received very little support. The Rump might not be popular, but there was no wish for another civil war.

The army and the Rump

With the defeat of Charles Stuart, the Rump gradually came under pressure from a different source – the army. While they were fully occupied in Scotland and Ireland and the threat of Royalism loomed, the politicised army were fairly quiet, supporting the Rump against common enemies. The Levellers, far from being a significant political element in the army, were driven underground, but the junior officers particularly still hoped for reforms. To a certain extent they were supported in this by the senior officers who were beginning to worry that the Rump would not disband themselves.

Law reform. One area that the army and some civilian reformers all thought needed attention was the law. The law was slow, old-fashioned (some of its procedures were even held in Norman French) and seemed to favour the rich. Under pressure from Cromwell, the Hale Commission on law reform was set up in 1651. It was to consider 'what inconveniences there are in the law . . . and the speediest way to reform the same'. However, the large group of lawyers in the Rump made sure that its recommendations were not taken up although procedures in court were changed to being in English. The important point is that the blocking of law reform made the Rump seem to be self-interested.

KEY THEME

The army's suspicion of the Rump In the spring of 1653 the Rump were preparing a bill for a 'new representative'. The army suspected that they would hold 'recruiter' elections' i.e. fill up the vacant seats while not standing for elections themselves, just carrying on sitting. The other suspicion was that they would 'vet' MPs who were elected, making sure they all got in themselves.

Political reform. Another area that aroused **the army's suspicion of the Rump** was that of the political future. Although the senior officers had rejected the radical proposals of the Levellers, they still saw the need for some reform. The leaders of the Rump ignored the army's calls for reform and gave the impression of being reluctant to call an election. In August 1652 the officers tried to dictate the day on which the Rump should dissolve and hold a new election, but Cromwell persuaded them not to push the matter to a conclusion.

The downfall of the Rump

Given the army's dissatisfaction with the Rump some kind of final showdown was inevitable. The army had become disillusioned with the Rump for the following reasons:

- Failure to bring in reforms.
- The belief that a civil war had been fought and a king executed just to make the world safe for Sir Arthur Heselrige and his group in the Rump, who were seen as enriching themselves and wishing to rule for ever.
- The Rump had been reluctant to allow religious toleration. They had rejected the scheme of John Owen (Cromwell's chaplain) to provide a framework of toleration for the more 'respectable' sects, while keeping down Ranters and the like. The scheme had also hoped to provide for an educated clergy.
- At the same time there were some in the army that were **Fifth Monarchists**. The group was led by Major General Thomas Harrison. He had contacts with Fifth Monarchists outside the army, especially a Welsh group led by Vasavour Powell who had a great deal of influence in the Commission for the Propagation of the Gospel in Wales.
- The Rump had failed to satisfy a wide variety of views within the army, and Heselrige had not made things any better by apparently preparing to remove Cromwell as Commander-in-Chief, and by treating the army with little consideration.

On 20 April 1653, when the Rump were debating a bill for a new representative, Cromwell ejected them using (significantly) Harrison's regiment to force them out of the

Major General Harrison.

The dissolution of the Rump.

Chamber. The army were now the masters and the public did not mourn the passing of the Rump.

OLIVER CROMWELL AND THE BAREBONES PARLIAMENT

Introduction
With the dismissal of the Rump, Cromwell became the key figure, and the army the real power in the land.

Cromwell's life
Born in 1599 in Huntingdon, Cromwell lived the life of a minor gentleman until the Civil War set him on the road to power. He sat in the 1628 Parliament and in the 1630s opposed the draining of the Fens which thus deprived poor Fen people of their livelihood on what had been common land. He was sarcastically called 'Lord of the Fens' by royal supporters. During the 1630s he also became converted to Puritanism and found himself in opposition to Bishop Wren, the Laudian Bishop of Ely. In 1642 he raised a troop of horse for Parliament and, by reason of his new-found talent for soldiering, rose to be commander of the Eastern Association cavalry.

Oliver Cromwell by Cooper.

Cromwell proved to be a soldier of genius, with an instinct about when to strike, and an enforcer of discipline. He grasped very early on that only professionalism could win wars although he had started as an amateur. By 1643 he had come up with (for the seventeenth century) a revolutionary principle – promotion by merit rather than birth: 'Give me your plain russet coated Captain who knows what he fights for . . . than your gentleman who is nothing else'. An Independent in religion, he seems to have promoted like-minded men and by 1648 had created, with Fairfax, a formidable military machine that in the 1650s was to be the most effective army in Europe. His control over an army that was professional, yet politically active, was based on two foundations:

• His remarkable series of victories from Marston Moor to Worcester, which gave him unparalleled trust and status with the troops.

- The fact that the army was, in many ways, his creation; the officers had a career 'open to their talents' through him. They were his creations and they enjoyed a life of status and potential promotion that would have been impossible to hope for in their former civilian lives. Many of the officers were sons of minor gentry but many were also from a lower station in life. Colonel Pride was (according to Royalist legend) a brewer's drayman, Major General Butler, the son of a butcher and grazier. Cromwellian officers were not, as Lord Clarendon the Royalist historian called them, 'Tinkers, button makers and dunghill operators', but they were from a lower social class than army officers were normally drawn from. In the last resort they knew that they owed their new-found power and status to Cromwell and therefore, whatever their reservations, they followed him.

Cromwell's character. Cromwell remained, in some of his attitudes, a typical Puritan country squire and MP. Therefore, he always tried to avoid becoming a military dictator, and sought to create viable civilian Parliamentary governments. It was those two sides to his make-up that help to explain some of the rather confusing twists and turns of his career:

- the 'conservative' country gentleman,
- the 'revolutionary' regicide soldier.

There are other aspects of Cromwell's personality and beliefs:

- He could suddenly act quite ruthlessly and take a new course that could be unpredictable, changing from 'conservative' to 'radical'.
- Cromwell's deep religious faith played a major part in his make-up. An important part of his religious thought was the idea that the English were God's chosen people. His one clear guiding principle was religious toleration – 'ideas will hurt no one but those that have them', and he intensely disliked religious persecution.
- Cromwell was the key figure of the 1650s; no one else could have performed the balancing act between the

army on one hand and the civilian gentry on the other, because only he had a 'foot in both camps'. He always had a loyalty to his old comrades in the army, yet understood the fear and dislike that military rule caused among the gentry.

- His great fear was anarchy and, given the situation in the 1640s and 1650s, this was understandable. He wished for a civilian government but the problem was that he had no clear ideas as to what form such a constitutional government might take – it would depend on circumstances. He once said: 'I am not wedded and glued to forms of government.'
- He did not trust many of the politicians such as Heselrige (who had been an ally of his in the 1640s) whose republican principles went hand-in-hand with the idea of a narrow group running the country. On the other hand, many of the traditional 'political nation' saw him as a regicide and so he could hope for little from them.

Views of Cromwell. In some ways, Cromwell remains a mystery.

- Clarendon, a Royalist, saw him as a 'Brave Bad Man'.
- Ludlow, a republican, as a schemer who perverted the Republic and took power for himself.
- The radicals, as the man who had the opportunity to bring in sweeping reforms and failed to do so.
- One of his coolest admirers, Andrew Marvell, the poet and MP, saw him almost as a force of nature and, at the same time, the only possible leader in an impossible time: 'If these be the times then this must be the man.'

Historians will continue to debate Cromwell's sincerity, his motivation and his successes and failures, but probably Marvell's summing up is a shrewd one. There were very many contradictions in Cromwell: his gentry and military sides, his sincere dislike of bigotry and persecution and, above all, his ability to control the army – all made him the only possible ruler in the confused society that was England in the 1650s. However, he was not consistent in what he did.

Oliver Cromwell by Robert Walker.

The Barebones or Little Parliament, April–December 1653

With the dismissal of the Rump, Cromwell and the Council of Officers found themselves the rulers of England. They faced certain problems.

- They had no wish to set up a military dictatorship but a straightforward general election might create a House of

Commons composed of Royalists, plus those conservative Parliamentarians excluded by Pride's Purge.
- All groups, including some of the republican Rumpers, hated the army. Any widely-elected parliament would launch an attack on the army, and the army, to defend their interests, might then have to conduct another purge.
- Yet military rule was unacceptable. Even the army wanted to have some form of civilian constitutional government provided it did not attack the army's interests, i.e. try to disband them, or fail to take their views into account.

The decision therefore was taken to have a nominated assembly, chosen by the army's Council of Officers. Influential in the Council of Officers with Cromwell was Thomas Harrison, who saw the new Parliament as an assembly of the godly. Harrison used his influence to have Fifth Monarchists and their sympathisers chosen. One of these was 'Praise God' Nicholas Barbon, from whom the nickname 'Barebones' came.

Cromwell's hopes for the Parliament
- Cromwell did share some of Harrison's vision and believed, for a while, that such an assembly of the godly would rule the English, God's chosen people, in a way directed by God.
- However, he had some very practical hopes for Barebones – he hoped for some law reform and for a dynamic preaching ministry which was 'a law ordered Ministry of learned and able divines bred at the universities'.
- Some of what Cromwell expected from the 'Little Parliament' with only 140 members was reflected in his speech at its opening with its language of religious enthusiasm, but the conservative side of his nature was also revealed when he talked of 'the stream of Government running in the old channel'.

The failure of Barebones. Given its **composition** – split between 'traditional' members and religious radicals – and the confused ideas behind its foundation, it is not surprising that the Parliament failed.

KEY THEME

Composition of the Barebones Parliament A picture has been drawn in the past of an assembly composed entirely of low-born religious extremists – Clarendon called them 'A pack of senseless fellows chosen for their gifts in praying and preaching', but actually the radicals were in the minority.

Austin Woolrych, in his *Commonwealth to Protectorate*, gives the following as the composition of the Commons: Greater gentry 17, Country gentry 22, Lesser gentry 66, out of a total of 144.

The majority of members were minor country gentry, the sort of people who had sat in previous parliaments, the only difference being most of them had never had any parliamentary experience. This may account for the fact that the radicals, although in the minority – probably at most only 60 members – were often able to dominate the assembly.

- **Reforms.** There were some sensible reforms. Civil marriage was introduced, as were legal measures to help debtors and creditors, and even regulations concerning the conditions under which lunatics were kept.
- **Religion.** However, in the matter of Church reform, a gap widened between the traditional members and the religious radicals. The radicals coordinated their efforts in Parliament by meeting at the house of Arthur Squibb, a radical member, to plan strategy. The traditional members were not used to organising themselves in Parliament, and sometimes did not appear for crucial votes, thus giving the radicals a free hand.

With these tactics the radicals succeeded in August in passing a vote to abolish the **Court of Chancery** without having anything to put in its place. In November and early December, they appeared to be making an all-out attack on the idea of any organised national Church structure or organisation.

- There were measures to abolish tithes without any thought of how the Church was to be financed, and the abolition of the **right of laymen to appoint to livings**. These were not only seen as tending towards dissolution of Church organisation but as an attack on property.
- At the same time there was an increase in the activities of the radical sects, and attacks on Cromwell who was seen by the religious visionaries as not supporting them. The army also came under attack with proposals that expenditure on it should be cut.
- In these circumstances the religious radicals had cut themselves off from support from anyone except themselves. Cromwell and many of the senior army officers, as well as moderates in the Parliament, were of the opinion that the Parliament had been hijacked by religious maniacs with no interest in settled government and the country was heading for chaos. Support for Fifth Monarchist ideas among the officers had waned, so Harrison was isolated in the Army Council.

The fall of Barebones. On 12 December 1653 the moderates staged a coup. While the Fifth Monarchists were holding an early morning prayer meeting at Squibb's

Court of Chancery Dealt with disputed legal cases, especially to do with inheritance of land. Often attacked for being very slow.

Right of laymen to appoint to livings A living was the term used to describe holding the ministry of a parish – the vicar or minister. Many gentry had the right to appoint the local minister to their church. This right could be left to others in a will and so was considered as a 'property'.

house as usual, the moderates turned up in force at Parliament and voted the Parliament out of existence. Rous, the Speaker, and a deputation then went to Whitehall and handed their power back to Cromwell. It only remained for the army to turn out the radicals when they arrived at the House of Commons. When the officer saw them sitting in the House he asked them why they were still there. They replied that they were praying – 'seeking the Lord'. 'Then you may go elsewhere', he said, 'because to my certain knowledge he has not been here these twelve years'.

SUMMARY QUESTIONS

1 Why did many people see religious radicalism as a threat? How much of a threat was it?

2 In your view, what were the two main weaknesses of the Rump Parliament? Explain your answer fully.

3 In your own words explain why the Barebones Parliament failed.

CHAPTER 8

The Protectorate, 1653–9

THE ESTABLISHMENT OF THE PROTECTORATE

The fall of the Barebones Parliament had, in theory, left England without a constitution or a government. In fact, behind the scenes some had been preparing for the moment when Barebones would fail. There had always been a group of army officers who had thought, not in terms of either a radical Leveller-influenced constitution or a **new Jerusalem** of rule by the 'saints', but a written constitution with moderate reforms that might command widespread support:

- It would allow civilian constitutional government.
- It would satisfy some demands for reform that dated back to the beginning of the Civil War.
- It would also give the army a permanent life as an accepted, settled part of government by laying down in law a permanent 'standing army'.

Lambert's role

The leading thinker behind this was Major General **John Lambert**. Lambert had withdrawn very early on from the Barebones Parliament and had drawn up a written constitution – the Instrument of Government. It is almost certain that he had contacts with the moderates in Parliament and, despite his denials, 'I knew not a tittle of this', Cromwell must have had some idea of Lambert's alternative constitutional scheme. Therefore, the coup of 12 December was not a despairing gesture by the moderates in Parliament. They knew that a new constitution was ready to be presented to Cromwell and that the majority of the Council of Officers would now be behind it. On 16 December 1653 Cromwell accepted the Instrument of Government and became Lord Protector.

John Lambert.

The Instrument of Government – main provisions

- The Lord Protector would be Head of State.
- The Lord Protector would be in control of the army with the consent of Parliament.
- A Council was named, with a system of replacing councillors in which Parliament had a part.
- Every male over 21 with either land or goods worth £200 should vote.
- A yearly revenue was established to support a standing army of 30,000 plus a navy.
- There was to be religious toleration for all except Anglicans and Catholics.
- There would be a permanent yearly sum of £200,000 to support the Protector's government.

The results of the Instrument. The Instrument, and the establishment of the Protectorate, can be seen as a move towards a more settled 'conservative' regime. But it did contain moderate reforms, e.g. some control of the executive (now Cromwell rather than Charles I) and some electoral reforms. In some ways it can be argued that, in the context of the situation of the 1650s, it was a sensible bid to produce a settlement. It was not just a swing towards conservatism, or a puppet constitution where the army pulled the strings. The reality of army power remained behind the scenes, however, and the success of the constitution depended on the Lord Protector being able to balance civilian and military interests.

ENGLAND UNDER THE PROTECTORATE, 1654–9

There were, of course, many who could not support the Protectorate, or who opposed it.

- Royalists saw it as a regicide regime, just as they had the Rump.
- Republicans, often called **Commonwealth's-men**, such as Heselrige, Scot, Vane and Ludlow, were opposed to any form of government with a 'single person' element. They had never forgiven Cromwell's military coup against the Rump and they were to be utterly opposed to him.

- The religious radicals, however, now saw Cromwell as 'the old dragon', 'the little horn of the great beast' – the man who had destroyed their chance of creating the 'new Jerusalem'.
- The political radicals did not see enough reforms of a fundamental kind in the Instrument. For them, the Protectorate was therefore a betrayal of the **Good Old Cause**, of reform for which the Civil War had been fought as far as they were concerned.

However, it remained to be seen how the vast majority of the political nation would accept the Instrument.

Cromwell's ordinances

The First Protectorate Parliament was due to be called in September 1654 and, in the meantime, Cromwell, with the Council of State, issued ordinances (instructions that became law) that were mainly sensible.

- The 'engagement' was withdrawn in the hope that more of the gentry would feel they could support the new regime if they did not have to swear oaths against their consciences.
- There were some moderate law reforms on the lines of the Hale Commission report, including regulating legal fees.
- To improve the standard of religious ministers, a board of commissioners, **the Triers**, was set up.
- County Committees of Ejectors were set up to remove incompetent schoolteachers.

In some cases these reforms did not have the effect that Cromwell had hoped for as, for instance, many objected to the activities of the Triers and Ejectors.

The Church under Cromwell

The loose state Church was the most tolerant in history. Individual congregations decided the form of worship in their parish and often chose their minister. Therefore, there was a wide degree of difference in worship between parishes.

KEY TERM

Good Old Cause This phrase was used by many who had fought for Parliament, especially the more radical. It meant rather different things to different people, but usually implied republicanism.

KEY THEME

The work of the Triers This was not supposed to impose conformity (Independents and Presbyterians were represented), but to ensure that ministers were educated and could preach. The resources of the Anglican Church, taken over during the Civil War, were used to give ministers higher stipends (salaries).

Religious toleration under Cromwell. England became the most religiously tolerant country in Europe under the Protectorate.

- Anglicans and Roman Catholics were, in practice if not in theory, allowed freedom of worship – a fact noted by the French ambassador.
- In 1655 the Jews, expelled from England in the 1290s, were readmitted.
- There were even some steps towards cooperation between differing religious groups such as Baxter's Worcestershire Association, which included moderate Anglicans, Presbyterians and Independents.
- However, the gentry's fear of some sects, such as the Ranters and the rapidly spreading Quakers, caused them to suffer intermittent persecution because they were seen as a threat to social order. Cromwell disliked such persecution and tried to prevent it when he could.

The First Protectorate Parliament, September 1654–January 1655

The Parliament ran into problems almost as soon as it met. Parliament immediately challenged the Protector's right to issue ordinances in the intervals between parliaments. The lawyers managed to overturn the law reforms, while the majority of members were suspicious of the army's powers. Cromwell took the line that the Instrument could not be changed by Parliament, and on 12 September he made MPs sign a 'Recognition' that they accepted the government as it was laid down by the Instrument. The Commonwealth's-men refused and withdrew from Parliament.

The failure of the First Protectorate Parliament. The absence of the likes of Heselrige, Vane, Bradshaw and Scot removed the leaders of opposition to the Protectorate but the arguing continued.

- The main target was the army. Parliament refused to pay for the army of over 50,000, wishing it cut down to the 30,000 laid down in the Instrument. They also wished to give control of the army to Parliament in the event of Oliver Cromwell's death.

- Cromwell was aware of the cost of the army and its unpopularity, and secretly he probably wished to reduce it to 30,000 (from 1655 onwards he gradually reduced its size) but he could not risk suddenly alienating the army by sacking over 20,000 officers and men.

Therefore, as soon as five lunar months (shorter than calendar months) had elapsed he dismissed Parliament on 22 January 1655.

Penruddock's Rising, March 1655

In the 1650s the government was very nervous of **Royalist conspiracy**. In fact, such conspiracy was fragmentary, reluctant and hyper-cautious even when it did exist. There was only one even moderately serious Royalist attempt during this period – the Penruddock Rising.

There had been some stirring among Royalists in the West Country but Cromwell's government had an efficient spy network; all letters posted in London were checked by one of **John Thurloe**'s agents who could recognise the handwriting of the leading Royalists. As a result when a signal for rebellion was given, many Royalist sympathisers were arrested. One group did actually rise in Wiltshire, led by John Penruddock, a minor gentleman. It was easily put down by Major General Desborough and twelve men were executed, the others being transported to the West Indies.

- Penruddock's Rising had failed largely because of preventative arrests and the reluctance of Royalists actually to commit themselves. However, the government seems to have taken fright, seeing Royalist conspiracy everywhere, and overreacted.

The Major Generals experiment, 1655–6

In the aftermath of the Penruddock Rising the decision was taken to divide England into eleven districts, each ruled by a Major General. The Major Generals had a formidable list of instructions and powers. They were to:

- set up a reliable militia (as some of the local forces had not supported the government during the Penruddock Rising);

KEY THEME

Royalist conspiracy Some secret Royalist societies existed but even the famous 'Sealed Knot' really spent most of their time drinking toasts to Charles II and doing very little. Royalist agents, such as Mordaunt, sent by Charles II from his exile in France and later the Spanish Netherlands, soon discovered how cautious Royalists actually were. Talk rather than action was the order of the day, as Royalist gentry had no wish to lose more of their estates through fines, or indeed their lives, in some hopeless uprising.

KEY PERSON

John Thurloe 1616–68
Lawyer, MP and Secretary to the Council of State. His real influence was that he was Cromwell's 'man of business' running the day-to-day affairs of the Protectorate and a very efficient information gathering service. He also ran Cromwell's secret service. Behind the scenes he was a vital figure.

John Thurloe.

- enforce the Poor Law;
- keep known Royalists under supervision;
- be guardians of public morality, closing brothels and gambling dens;
- suppress unlawful assemblies;
- make sure the local JPs carried out their duties effectively;
- collect the 10 per cent Decimation Tax on Royalist estates that was to finance the whole scheme.

The Major Generals were sometimes Puritan killjoys who used their powers to stop the population having innocent pleasures, and were seen as agents of military rule. They are the basis for the legend of grim Puritan dictatorship that has been associated with the Cromwellian regime.

The varied attitudes of the Major Generals. The Major Generals varied in their popularity and approach.

- Worsley in Lancashire seems to have been the classic Puritan bigot whose obsession was closing alehouses.
- Butler in Northamptonshire used his powers to blackmail Royalist gentry, imprison Quakers and make enough money to build Cobthorne in Oundle, one of the finest mid-seventeenth-century houses in England.

Other Major Generals were hardworking men who made an effort to get on with the local gentry and helped the poor. However, they all became 'tarred with the same bush' of arrogant military dictatorship.

The effect of the Major Generals. Establishing the Major Generals did more to alienate the traditional gentry 'political nation' from the Protectorate than any other move. In terms of 'healing and settling' – a theme that Cromwell was to take up increasingly – it was a disaster, the memory of which haunted the regime to the end. 'The most intolerable regime England ever had', remarked one country gentleman. The county gentry deeply resented their local power and influence being taken away from them by soldiers who were often seen as members of the 'lower orders' and dictators.

The Second Protectorate Parliament, September 1656–February 1658

From the outset this Parliament was determined to be rid of the Major Generals. The army who had influenced Cromwell into calling Parliament did not seem to realise its unpopularity. Many of the Major Generals never realised the deep loathing that they created among the gentry. Butler, for instance, had allied himself with Sir Gilbert Pickering in Northamptonshire to pressurise the voters to return him and Sir Gilbert to Parliament. In the event, Butler only narrowly escaped being legally tried by Parliament for corruption and Cromwell hastily abandoned the Major Generals experiment.

With the fall of the Major Generals, Cromwell began moving in a conservative direction while trying to save the gains, as he saw them, of the republican years including religious tolerance. A case in point was that of **James Naylor**.

Over 100 MPs had been excluded from the first session of the Parliament as being opponents of the Instrument and the Protectorate. It was the conservatives in Parliament, now in the majority, who came up with the obvious move towards the old and known constitutional ways – they offered Cromwell the Crown. This offer was contained in a constitutional plan known as the Humble Petition and Advice. The main movers of this scheme were Broghill, Cromwell's ally in Ireland, and Sir Richard Onslow, a Surrey MP. Cromwell was, after some thought, to refuse it.

Why did Cromwell refuse the Crown?

- Cromwell seemed to waver. One side of his nature had always wanted the old constitution (with safeguards and reforms) and, if the evidence of Bulstrode Whitlocke, a man of changing principles, is to be relied on, Cromwell had as early as 1652 posed the question: 'What if a man should take it on himself to be King?'
- Kingship was the known traditional form of government. Gentry who were not fanatical Royalists attached to the House of Stuart would probably accept King Oliver. Edward Hyde, later the Earl of Clarendon, Charles II's closest adviser abroad, actually thought that

The case of James Naylor
Cromwell bitterly opposed the punishment of James Naylor, a Quaker who had entered Bristol on a donkey in imitation of Jesus Christ's entry into Jerusalem. The gentry of the Second Protectorate Parliament saw him as a dangerous blasphemer. Cromwell on the other hand regarded him as a deluded, harmless man but he was powerless to prevent Parliament punishing Naylor for blasphemy and having him branded and imprisoned. Cromwell could not force people to be tolerant.

Charles Fleetwood.

if Cromwell had accepted the Crown, Stuart Royalism would be doomed.

KEY THEME

The Humble Petition and Advice

Main points:

• The Protector could name his successor.
• There was to be an 'Upper House' of 40.
• Officers of State and Councillors to be approved by Parliament.
• Parliament to meet every two years.

KEY PERSON

Charles Fleetwood
1618–92 Oliver Cromwell's son-in-law Fleetwood was Commander-in-Chief in Ireland 1652–7. He was a Baptist (Baptists believe in adult baptism to wash away sin) and he built up a following among Baptists in the army. Not a very strong figure, Fleetwood may have been chosen by Cromwell in 1657 to be Commander-in-Chief of the army so that Cromwell could have the real power. Eventually Fleetwood opposed Richard Cromwell but fell from power in December 1659 as he was unable to hold the army together.

There were, however, strong reasons both personal and political behind Cromwell's refusal.

• The army had elements in it that would never accept kingship again – it would be the ultimate betrayal of the 'Good Old Cause'. Cromwell would have faced an army revolt.
• Personally, Cromwell had been the prime mover behind the execution of the King so it would be an act of total hypocrisy to accept the Crown.
• Cromwell seems to have decided that kingship was a form of government which God, by granting him all his victories, had 'witnessed against'. It was a corrupt form of government: 'I would not build **Jericho** again', he said.

The Humble Petition and Advice, 1657. When Cromwell refused the Crown, the **Humble Petition and Advice** was revised and the right of the Protector to name his successor was substituted. Cromwell accepted the revised scheme in March 1657, although the Humble Petition was not popular with some elements in the army.

• **Fleetwood**, the Commander-in-Chief and Cromwell's son-in-law, seems to have threatened to resign but, typically, did not.
• Lambert, whose hopes of being the next Protector were now shattered (as Cromwell would probably nominate one of his own sons), was forced to resign but with a very large pension.
• Colonel Packer and five captains resigned their commissions, but the army in general remained quiet, if puzzled and resentful.
• Some of the senior officers probably hoped that as they had places in the new Upper House they could make sure that the army's interests would be protected against attacks by gentry MPs.

The second session. In the second session of the Parliament, some of the Commonwealth's-men, such as

Heselrige, were readmitted. They immediately attacked the Humble Petition. Parliament broke up into factions with Heselrige and his supporters trying to force a vote to bring down the Protectorate and restore the Rump. The vote was due to be held on 4 February 1658, and although it was by no means sure that it would pass, and would have no force if it did, Oliver Cromwell decided to act. He dissolved Parliament, saying to the republican Commonwealth's-men, 'Let God choose between you and me.' They replied, 'Amen.'

The last months of Oliver Cromwell's Protectorate

Cromwell faced great problems, and in some ways they showed up the weakness of the whole system. Cromwell seems to have become more depressed and ill; George Fox, the Quaker, spoke of seeing him at Hampton Court with 'a waft of death' about him. On 3 September, the anniversary of his great victories at Dunbar and Worcester, he died, during a violent thunderstorm. He had chosen his eldest son Richard as the next Lord Protector.

The situation at Cromwell's death

- Cromwell had not really prepared his eldest son Richard to succeed him, only bringing him into the Council during the last months.
- Aware of the potential unrest in the army, Oliver was preparing to 'purge' unreliable officers who would not support the Protectorate. He died before they could be removed. This would be important for the security of Richard Cromwell.
- Public debt meant that the army would, in any case, have to be further reduced in size.
- Despite these problems there was no prospect of the Restoration of Charles II. Royalists, even with the key figure of the Republic dead, did nothing. Therefore, Thurloe, writing to Henry, Oliver's younger son in Ireland, remarked: 'Not a dog stirs amongst us.' And Hyde thought Cromwell's 'power and greatness . . . better established than ever' at the moment of his death.

Therefore the **survival of the Protectorate** would depend on Richard's skill in controlling the political ambitions of the army, while 'healing and settling' the traditional

KEY THEME

Survival of the Protectorate The regime was deeply in debt and the country was still divided – Royalists, republicans, conservatives and radicals – the Protectorate had not resolved those differences. In addition, the army resented the new powers and almost monarchical status of the Protector.

political nation. The Protectorate was not automatically doomed at the death of Oliver.

SUMMARY QUESTION

1 What do you think were the aims behind the Instrument of Government?

CHAPTER 9

Interregnum foreign policy

THE RUMP, 1649–53

The Council of State of the Rump found itself faced with many problems in 1650:

- a potential Royalist conspiracy;
- threats (however vague) from the radicals in the army and in the country at large who expected great changes as a result of the Parliamentary victory in two civil wars and the execution of the King;
- Royalist activity/threats from Scotland and Ireland.

The Council of State therefore found itself in a difficult position. The Rump had to assert its authority over England, Scotland and Ireland, while containing potential threats from its opponents in England. In theory, therefore, foreign policy should have been purely a matter of survival. The Rump needed allies.

FOREIGN ATTITUDES TO THE REPUBLIC

The execution of Charles I, executed not as a 'backstairs' murder (that had happened to English kings before) but as an 'enemy of the people' – tried by a court and publicly executed – sent shock-waves throughout Europe. It must be remembered that to execute a king publicly and set up a Republic (however conservative its aims actually were) was a shocking act to European monarchies. The Rump was seen as a dangerous 'revolutionary' regime in the same way as republican France after 1793 or Russia after 1917. The Rump was potentially isolated in Europe. At first only Spain recognised the regicide Republic – almost certainly for reasons of political power – in the hope of gaining an ally or a neutral 'friend' against France.

THE RUMP'S ATTITUDE TO EUROPE

KEY TERM

The United Provinces
What would be called the
Low Countries, i.e. parts of
the Netherlands and Belgium,
the United Provinces were
divided into states and
governed by the House of
Orange. For many members
of the Rump, the United
Provinces were a fellow
Protestant, republican regime,
so England and the United
Provinces had the same
interests – the defeat of
Roman Catholic absolutist
forces in Europe.

In some ways the Rump had an 'old-fashioned' attitude to
European politics in 1650. Parliament in 1642 had seen
their natural ally as being the **United Provinces** because
they were Protestant.

The St John Mission, 1651. As early as 1642 Walter
Strickland had been sent by Parliament to create good
relations and 'a closer union' between England and the
United Provinces. It had not been a success because the
Stadholder of the Provinces, William II of Orange (in real
terms a president/monarch figure), had sympathies for, and
was related to, the Stuarts. With his death in 1650, it
seemed that there was a real chance of a change in
sympathy. In February 1651 the Rump sent Oliver St John
and Strickland to offer the States General (the ruling
council of the eight Provinces) a 'Union' between the two
Protestant republics. The Rump Council of State believed
that, with the influence of William II removed, the
Protestant Provinces would welcome such a move. They
rejected it, and the St John Mission was publicly insulted.

Why did the United Provinces reject Union?
- The Provinces did not have the same attitudes as the
  republican English. Some states of the United Provinces
  were strongly opposed to the new regime in England,
  supporting the House of Orange and its Stuart
  sympathisers.
- The United Provinces were not a very tight-knit group
  who would always have the same interests: the States
  General consisted of eight provinces, seven of which had
  equal voting rights. There were divisions among the
  Provinces on many issues and the States General was not
  a centralised government like the English Rump.
- The United Provinces had just made peace with Spain in
  1650 so did not need English help to maintain their
  independence.
- There was a feeling among the Dutch that union with
  England, a much larger country, would mean loss of
  independence as England would swallow up the United
  Provinces.

- The Dutch saw the English as trade rivals hoping to take over Dutch trade.

So, for the United Provinces, the fact that the English Republic was Protestant was not the main issue. Some Dutch were even suspicious of the 'extreme' Protestantism (as they saw it) of the republicans in England. To the United Provinces, trade and independence were more important than religious considerations. At first, the Rump did not understand this.

THE NAVIGATION ACT, 1651

The Rump had set up a Council of Trade to 'maintain and advance the traffic trade and several manufacturers of this nation'.

Causes of the Navigation Act

- From the beginning of the Republic there was a group of merchants who were anxious to break the Dutch hold on the 'carrying trade' – the carrying of cargoes by the huge Dutch merchant navy – and the power of the Dutch East India Company, the VOC.
- They saw opportunities for English trade and English shipping and resented the Dutch stranglehold over trade, not only in European waters but in the Far East.
- They still resented the VOC's violent resistance of the English East India Company's attempts to carve out a trading empire in the East – which had, at one point, resulted in the Amboina Massacre of 1623 when the Dutch had murdered English traders.
- For this group, religion was not the issue. Like the Dutch, trade was the priority.

The Act. When the St John Mission returned humiliated and empty handed, the Rump turned against the United Provinces. The result was the Navigation Act which laid down that all goods coming to England, Scotland, Ireland or English colonies should come in English vessels, or in vessels belonging to the original country of origin of the goods. This was a direct challenge to the Dutch 'carrying trade' as the Dutch had a near monopoly of carrying goods to Scotland and the English colonies in North America. The English claimed the right to search Dutch ships to ensure that the Navigation Act was not being evaded by the Dutch.

THE FIRST DUTCH WAR, 1652–4

The Navigation Act was the trigger for a war that perhaps many in both the United Provinces and England did not really want.

- The Dutch made a rather vague effort to negotiate, sending Jacob Cats, a possibly mad poet, to London. He addressed the Council of State in Dutch verse, which they did not understand.
- At the same time, the States General ordered a fleet of 150 ships to be ready to resist English demands to stop and search Dutch ships. This was seen by the Rump as a declaration of war.
- The actual outbreak of hostilities occurred at the end of May 1652 when the Dutch admiral Tromp refused to salute the English flag in English waters (an accepted practice) and he and the English admiral **Robert Blake** opened fire on each other. The matter of saluting the flag was the excuse – the first Anglo-Dutch war had been brewing for a year.

The course of the war. The advantage lay with the English in the First Dutch War.

- They were attacking rich Dutch merchant convoys but the English merchant ships did not present such a large or rich target for Dutch ships. As one Dutch official remarked: 'The English are attacking a mountain of gold, we are attacking a mountain of iron.'
- The Dutch had to pass through the English Channel or go around the north of Scotland, a very dangerous voyage, so the strategic advantage lay with the English.
- English warships were larger and more heavily armed. Although they could not get into the shallow waters around the coast of Holland, in the open sea they were superior to Dutch warships.

A series of English victories was the result of these advantages, partly helped by the death of the best of the Dutch admirals, Tromp, at the Battle of the Texel in August 1653. By the end of 1653 the Dutch had lost over 1000 ships, to the English losses of 300, and the Dutch coast was being blockaded (closed to ships) by the English. The Dutch were ready to make peace and, with Cromwell installed as Lord Protector in December 1653, English foreign policy took a new turn.

Cromwell's foreign policy. The Barebones Parliament had been even more anxious than the Rump to continue the war against the Dutch. They regarded the Dutch as Protestants who had become corrupted by wealth and had strayed from 'true religion'. **Cromwell, however, saw it differently.**

The Treaty of Westminster, April 1654. This treaty ended the First Dutch War.

- The Dutch agreed to accept the Navigation Act.
- They agreed to salute the English flag in English waters.
- To Cromwell the most important clause of the Treaty was that the Dutch agreed not to allow any English Royalists to live in the United Provinces.

Prestige of England. The defeat of Holland gave the Protectorate status in Europe, status that was to increase in the next few years. England seemed to have become a real power.

THE WAR WITH SPAIN, 1654–9

The 'Western Design' – war against Spain in the West Indies. Cromwell decided to use the huge English fleet to attack Spain in the New World. In December 1654 a fleet and army were sent to capture Hispaniola (Haiti). The commander General Venables was not perhaps the most dynamic of soldiers and he argued with the admiral Penn. The food and equipment were not well organised and the tropical conditions caused terrible losses from disease. The attack failed but Jamaica was captured. In the long run it

KEY THEMES

Cromwell's attitude to the war To Cromwell the Dutch were 'fellow Protestants'. England's real enemies were Catholic countries, especially Spain. He did not want to see a potential ally against Spain completely crushed. Cromwell was not prepared to repeal the Navigation Act, because he could see the advantages to English trade, but he did want to close down the war.

Arguments for and against the peace

Against: Cromwell was criticised for letting the Dutch get an easy peace. Slingsby Bethel argued in his famous pamphlet *England's Mistake in Oliver Cromwell* that Cromwell had missed a golden opportunity to crush the Dutch and make English trade supreme.

For: On the other hand, had Cromwell continued the war, the cost would have been very great. If England had completely defeated the Dutch at sea, Thurloe thought that the States General might have been overthrown and a pro-Royalist Orange party would have taken power. By making peace, Cromwell secured the Protectorate against Royalist exiles operating from Holland.

was an important strategic base, but at the time it was not seen as of great significance. Cromwell was not discouraged and continued with the war, despite the very high cost in taxation.

The French alliance. In March 1657 Cromwell entered into an **alliance with France**. Part of this alliance was an agreement for a joint attack on the Spanish Netherlands. English troops showed what a formidable army the Protector had created at Mardyke in October 1657 and at the Battle of the Dunes in June 1658. Royalist exiles fought for the Spanish, while the French admired the professionalism and discipline of the English 'Redcoats' fighting for the Protectorate. Many Royalists were demoralised by the efficiency of Cromwell's troops. As a result of the alliance, Dunkirk was given to England. It was an important port but, even more vital, it had been full of pirates and Royalist ships preying on English shipping.

THE BALTIC

The Baltic area was of great importance to England, not only because of English trade to Scandinavia, but because much of the timber needed to build English ships came from there. Cromwell's main concern was to ensure that the Sound, the entrance to the Baltic, was always kept open to English ships. This he did by supporting Charles X of Sweden, thus putting pressure on the Danes and their allies, the Dutch. Sweden, at this time, was the most important power in the Baltic area but the support of the English navy made sure that Charles X could dominate it and keep the Sound open.

CONCLUSION

- Cromwell's foreign policy has been attacked as being 'out of date', as being anti-Spanish when the rising power was France; he should have kept France 'under control' rather than allying with it against Spain.
- However, whatever mistakes Cromwell may have made, England was seen as a great power under the

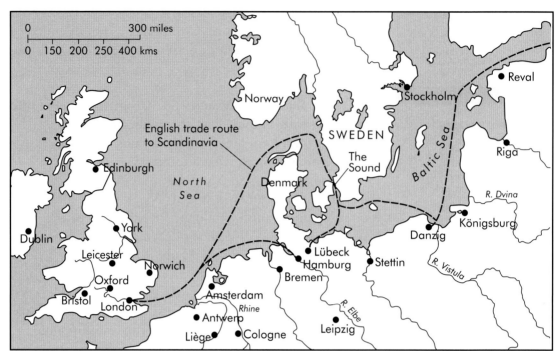

The Baltic area in the 1650s.

Protectorate, and many countries were anxious to be friendly with the Protectorate. In 1640 there were three foreign ambassadors in London, by 1658 there were 20. Clarendon said of Cromwell: 'His greatness at home, was but a shadow of his greatness abroad.'

SUMMARY QUESTION

1 What were the sucesses and failures of Cromwell's foreign policy?

A2: ANALYSIS AND INTERPRETATION

SECTION 3

The English Republic

WHY BY DECEMBER 1653 HAD OLIVER CROMWELL BECOME LORD PROTECTOR?

Key themes

There are a number of factors which explain the collapse of the Rump Parliament and the decision of Cromwell to become Lord Protector.

- The role of the army was crucial to this process as was the attitude of the political nation.
- Cromwell himself was to play a key role in the process.

The desire for stability. The leading Rumpers, Sir Arthur Heselrige, Sir Henry Vane and Thomas Scot, were convinced republicans, believing that the execution of the King was not only just but justified as it enabled England to become a republic – the best form of government. These men were not revolutionaries in the political or social sense, although even to agree to execute the King was, of course, 'revolutionary' in seventeenth-century terms. They were gentry concerned to preserve property against the power of absolutist monarchs. All monarchs would tend, they argued, to extend their powers and therefore threaten the property of their subjects, so monarchy must go. However, republicanism for them was about stability, the rule of law and the social hierarchy. Some Rumpers had come to accept the execution of Charles because he *was* Charles, untrustworthy and dangerous. For them execution was a sad necessity. Other Rumpers were sitting only to ensure the interests of their constituents and to keep government going.

Attitude of the gentry to the Rump. For many of the traditional gentry, Royalist or Parliamentarian, the execution of the King had been an unforgivable act – an act that tarred the Rump from the beginning. However, the administration of the counties had to go on, government had to function. So some, as long as they were not forced into agreement with the execution, might have been prepared to serve the Rump as the temporary government in order to prevent anarchy. However, the 'engagement' of 1650 forced them, if they were prepared to take office, to accept the Rump as permanent government. This was too much for many and the Rump never had the full cooperation of the majority of the political nation.

The army and the Rump. If, however, the Rump had had the full support of the 50,000-strong army then it could have survived against the passive or active dislike of the traditional political nation. The army's attitude to the Rump was always one of grudging support. The army was, of course, republican, so there was no question of Royalist support anywhere in the army. However, the rather conservative republicanism of Heselrige was not the sort that many in the army felt they had fought a civil war for. The rest of the Rump remained suspicious of the army and of its demands for reform. This suspicion was based on three counts:

- Firstly, the Rump was well aware of the cost of the army, and wished, if it could, to bring down taxation. By 1653 there was a deficit of £700,000. The Rumpers realised that the now professional army would not take kindly to being cut down in size. 'Redundancies' in the army would mean officers going back to less well-paid and prestigious positions in civilian life.
- Secondly, conservative Rumpers had never forgotten the army radicalism in 1647–8, and knew that these ideals had not been totally eliminated, they had gone underground.
- Thirdly, the more astute saw the army as a potential rival for political power. Very few Rumpers were supporters of the army in these circumstances – most of the time only the radical republican, Sir Henry Marten, tried actively to keep lines of communication open to the army.

For the army's part, many saw the Rump as an institution full of men who had **profited from the revolution**. The Rump always appeared hesitant in matters of reform – law reform and religion in particular. Many in the army looked back to some of the clauses in the Heads of Proposals as a possible new constitution, while the more radical, in political terms, still held Leveller ideas. With the end of the war in Scotland and Ireland, the implied threat to the Rump from the army became concrete. No longer was the army occupied in fighting the Republic's enemies, they could now turn their attention to what sort of a Republic they wanted. Unlike the Rump the army did not see the present constitutional set-up as permanent.

The role of Cromwell. Oliver Cromwell, Commander-in-Chief ever since Fairfax's retirement in 1650, became the key figure. His status in the army, as the commander who had partly created the army and then led it to its remarkable series of victories, made him the only man who could

KEY THEME

Profiting from the revolution
The idea that the Rump was full of men who had profited from the revolution was not altogether unfair. Sir Arthur Heselrige made large sums out of coalfields that had formerly belonged to the Bishop of Durham.

hold the various groups in the army together. Some leading Rumpers already saw Cromwell's power and feared it.

Politics in the army. Hard-line political radicalism on Leveller lines was really only an attitude held by some of the junior officers. Many officers favoured some form of written constitution with moderate reforms, hence the support for aspects of the Heads of Proposals.

- The most influential of these officers, after the death of Henry Ireton in 1652, was John Lambert. He saw the future in terms of a reformed constitution which would protect various interests in the nation, including the army's.
- Directly opposed to this view of the future was Major General Harrison with his Fifth Monarchist views. To Harrison, paper constitutions were not the issue – the godly must rule God's chosen people.

Neither of these opposing views on the Army Council had any time for the Rump. However, without Cromwell's support neither side could hope to sway the army into action. The soldiers would follow Cromwell. Neither Lambert nor Harrison had a strong enough following to act without Cromwell's support.

The fall of the Rump. In the light of Heselrige's attempt to remove Oliver Cromwell and Cromwell's belief that the Rump would make itself a 'perpetual Parliament', the Rump's days were numbered. No one in the army would support the continuation of the Rump, and the army would follow where Cromwell led.

At this point Cromwell appears to have been influenced by his strong feeling that the English were 'God's people' and, although he did not share all Harrison's eccentric religious visions, he had sympathy for his viewpoint. It is always difficult to be precise about Cromwell's views and motivation at any point in his career, but it could be argued that allied to his sympathy for some of Harrison's vision was the general feeling of unease that he felt about the Rump. Perhaps Cromwell felt a great civil war had been fought, the King had been executed and what was the result? The world had been made safe for Sir Arthur Heselrige. He certainly did not share the Levellers' view of the future, but he probably thought that some reforms should happen. Instead, he was faced with a group of Rumpers who appeared to be interested only in their own survival.

It is impossible to know exactly what Cromwell's motives were when, on 20 April 1653, he closed down the Rump, using Harrison's own regiment. With the fall of the Rump all real power rested with Cromwell and the Council of Officers.

Cromwell's disappointment with the Barebones Parliament. The Council of Officers and Cromwell were reluctant to rule as a military dictatorship. On the other hand, free elections might result in a Parliament that would be against the army's interests and against reform – religious or political. With the fall of the Rump, all power rested in Cromwell's hands, but with the mixture of the conservative country gentlemen and the religious enthusiasts he decided on an assembly of the godly – the Barebones, Nominated or Little Parliament.

Its composition reflected both Cromwell's attitudes and those of the Council of Officers. Many of the officers were not supporters of Harrison's visionary schemes for a 'new Jerusalem' ruled by a group of the godly modelled on the Jewish Sanhedrin of 70. Cromwell himself wanted a larger body – 140 was the final figure and many of those nominated by the Council of Officers were the sort of gentry who had served in previous parliaments. Cromwell's reluctance to completely fall in with Harrison's ideas casts doubt on the idea that he was in some kind of religious trance, influenced totally by the Fifth Monarchists and other religious radicals.

Nevertheless, he seems to have had high hopes of the new assembly when it opened on 4 July 1653. In the event he was to be disappointed and by December 1653 had come to regard the radicals in the Barebones Parliament as a menace to stability. Some of the officers who were members of the Barebones also took fright. Lambert had a written constitution already prepared when the conservatives in the Barebones Parliament surrendered their power to Cromwell on 12 December. Those who did so were conservatives hoping that Cromwell would produce stability rather than 'the confusion of all things', as Cromwell was to describe the rule of Barebones.

Cromwell, at this point, was looking for a settlement that would have within it moderate reforms plus stability – the essentials of the 'revolution' preserved, but the rule of law and the 'old ways' returned to. The Instrument of Government, based on Lambert's draft constitution, seemed to promise this.

Conclusion
- Cromwell was the only possible choice as Lord Protector. He could control the army, yet sympathised with some of its aspirations and aims. Therefore only he could provide the chance of a settlement which could keep the army quiet, yet make moves towards the traditional political nation.
- At the time he was, in some ways, the typical 'parliamentary country gentleman' Puritan, concerned with law and order and stability. No one else could fill this role in December 1653. There were many

country gentlemen of prominence but they themselves were divided by religion, politics and the execution of Charles I.

- Whether or not his unique position with a foot in both camps could provide a lasting settlement was another matter, but no one else was in this unique position and could even try.

WHY WAS THERE NO LASTING SETTLEMENT IN THE 1650s?

Introduction: The quest for settlement
The central theme of the period 1649–60 is the attempt to produce a settlement that the majority of the political nation could, however reluctantly, adopt.

Key themes
- The shortness of the time span is important: the Protectorate lasted only five and a half years. With time it might have proved a durable government. The Instrument of Government and the Humble Petition and Advice were by no means unreasonable attempts at settlement.
- The character of Richard Cromwell meant that he could not create a viable settlement because he could not control the army, the hated organisation that had ridden roughshod over the traditional political nation (see Part 3).
- The Rump, restored in 1659, was quite unable to produce a settlement. Unpopular in the period 1650–3, it failed to understand the aspirations and attitudes of its enemies on 'the right' – the traditional Royalist and Presbyterian members who had been excluded – or the army (see Part 3).
- Perhaps only 'limited' monarchy could heal the wounds and divisions of the past 20 years, and the Interregnum showed that. There could be no settlement without the consent of the traditional gentry. Their consent was at most grudging to Oliver Cromwell, and they were powerless to support Richard. They could never give support to the Commonwealth's-men of the Rump and, as the anarchy of the winter of 1659–60 showed very clearly, only the 'old constitution' could provide stability (see Part 3).
- The Royalists argument was that there could be no lasting settlement, as the 'natural' government acceptable to the majority of the political nation was monarchy with certain curbs on the monarch's powers. No other political settlement was 'natural' or would have widespread support. Royalists, during the Interregnum and after the Restoration of Charles II, naturally took this line, as have many historians.

The Royalist line examined. If the Royalist line of argument is taken, the Commonwealth and Protectorate governments were doomed from the start because their support base in the country at large was too narrow.

Even Parliamentarians such as Sir Charles Broghill, Sir Richard Onslow and others opposed to a Stuart restoration had, by 1657, come to the conclusion that a 'mixed' monarchy with king, House of Lords and House of Commons was the way forward to a settlement but the king would be Oliver Cromwell. Even Cromwell himself seems, at times, to have wanted a monarchy.

An illustration of the difficulties: an exchange between Cromwell and Edmund Ludlow

Edmund Ludlow was a regicide republican and a gentleman who had been a Colonel during the First Civil War and a Lieutenant General in Ireland in the early 1650s. He admired Ireton's honesty and was a convinced republican. Ludlow refused to accept the Protectorate, seeing it as a betrayal of the 'Good Old Cause'. He helped to engineer the fall of Richard Cromwell in 1659 and tried, unlike Heselrige, at last to understand the army's point of view during the rule of the restored Rump.

Cromwell asked Ludlow: 'What would you have?' Ludlow's reply was: 'I would have what we fought for, that the nation be governed by its own consent.' Cromwell's reply illustrated the problems of the Interregnum: 'But where is that consent to be found?' Cromwell went on to list the various factions that had developed as a result of the Civil Wars.

If the Royalist view is correct then it was a fruitless quest for settlement. However, it can be argued that the Royalist view is not altogether proven.

- Certainly Royalists in the 1650s were not dynamic in their opposition to the republican regimes. Even after the death of Cromwell in September 1658, they remained quiet and, to the despair of Royalist exiles, the Protectorate seemed secure.
- The fall of Richard in May 1659, and the restoration of the Rump, did not lead to a restoration of the monarchy. It was not until the winter of 1659–60, as the forces opposed to Restoration disintegrated, particularly the army arguing among themselves, that Restoration was possible.

Because Restoration came in 1660 it does not necessarily mean that it was inevitable.

What were the obstacles to settlement? The quest for settlement in the 1650s was made difficult because, by 1650, the political nation had been transformed. In 1642 most influence and power was held by the county gentry; by 1650 a whole new political spectrum existed. The political nation of 1650 was composed of far more groups and was much larger than that of 1642. Therefore, England was much more difficult to govern in the 1650s.

Conclusion

To construct a system of government that would satisfy the aspirations of the Presbyterians, Independents, political radicals, Royalists, religious radicals, the army and the traditional county gentry was an almost impossible task. Perhaps reluctant acceptance was the most that could be hoped for.

WHY WERE SOME GROUPS OPPOSED TO THE REGIMES OF THE 1650s AND HOW SIGNIFICANT A THREAT DID THEY POSE?

Key themes

There was a variety of reasons why different groups opposed the regimes of the 1650s. However, the threat they posed was, for the most part, limited.

How significant were the Royalists in the 1650s?

For some who had fought for Charles and suffered for it, nothing save the restoration of the rightful king, Charles II, would be acceptable. They would not be reconciled to any government save a Royal Stuart one. However, the actual number of totally committed Royalists can be exaggerated. As the 1650s wore on, some Royalists became convinced that restoration of the monarchy was impossible and tried to come to terms with that. Ex-Royalists, such as Thomas, Earl Fauconberg even married into the Protector's family, and Richard Cromwell had Royalist friends.

Isolation and failure of the Royalists. The failure of Penruddock's Rising in 1655 showed many Royalists how hopeless their cause was. Some diehard Royalists refused to consider any alliance with other opponents of the Protectorate. Booth's Rebellion in the summer of 1659, against a Rump that was by no means popular, did not attract much Royalist support. This was even though Booth was calling for a 'Free Parliament' – new elections that might favour Royalist candidates and therefore indirectly lead to Restoration. Sir George Booth was a Presbyterian who had fought against Charles I in the First Civil War and many Royalists would have nothing to do with him. So Royalists cut themselves off from potential allies among the conservative gentry who, like them, had been appalled at the execution of Charles and, like them, deeply disliked a regicide republic.

The Secluded (excluded) Members

The Secluded Members is another name for the excluded members, the majority of the old Long Parliament ousted by Colonel Pride in 1648. They saw the army's interference with the rights of Parliament as monstrous, and the execution of the King as a shocking illegal act. Some of the excluded members did decide to make peace with the Rump but many, such as William Prynne, regarded all regimes in the 1650s as illegal, because of Pride's Purge. However, they could not make common cause with the diehard Royalists because they were viewed with suspicion as being responsible for starting a civil war against Charles and therefore being responsible for the disasters that followed. As conservative Presbyterians, however much they rejected the Republic, they believed that the Royalist aims of a restoration of Charles II without any terms imposed on him was unacceptable.

Republicans

Republicans such as Lucy Hutchinson were affronted by the Protectorate, despite her contempt for 'mean fellows' as she called some of Cromwell's officers. Edmund Ludlow, son of an old Wiltshire gentry family, might have shared some of Lucy Hutchinson's social attitudes, although he had some sympathy for the radicals, but he too was a convinced republican and to him Cromwell was an apostate or traitor from the 'Good Old Cause' and a 'usurper'.

The political radicals

Some radicals, suspicious of the Rump from the start, did originally look to Cromwell. Gerard Winstanley, leader of the Diggers, addressed his pamphlets to Cromwell, but for most radicals Cromwell and the gentry-dominated Rump were intent on betraying the 'Good Old Cause'. By 1649 Cromwell had seen the Levellers as a threat to order in potentially dangerous times. He told the Council of State: 'You have no other way to deal with these men but to break them.' Lilburne had published 'an impeachment of High Treason against Oliver Cromwell and his son-in-law Henry Ireton' and, despite being tried for sedition and acquitted, Lilburne was kept in custody by the Rump and the Protectorate until 1657.

How much of a threat were the Levellers? By 1650 it can be argued that the **Levellers** were not a real threat. Firstly, the majority of the army were more concerned with pay and conditions than theoretical schemes of government. When in 1649 Cromwell and Ireton persuaded the Rump to pay the monies owing to the troops, much of the army lost interest in political reform on a large scale, as opposed to some moderate changes. Also, the anarchy of 1647 and the bad harvests had increased public discontent; with stability seeming to return, the Levellers lost much of their appeal. As important, was their lack of support among the senior

KEY THEME

The destruction of the Levellers
On 14 May 1649 Cromwell crushed the Leveller mutinies in the army at Burford in Oxfordshire. With the destruction of the Levellers within the army, the movement had no further chance of success. Levellerism remained an 'attitude of mind' among some of the junior officers, to resurface after the fall of the Protectorate, but it had no real power base.

officers and in Parliament. They had no powerful advocates where power ultimately rested.

To a certain extent, the often-used phrase 'Leveller movement' seems to indicate a degree of organisation that was simply not there. Levellers disagreed among themselves about the Leveller programme; some Levellers took the line that 'all should vote', others would have excluded servants and those dependent on parish charity, i.e. those who could not be trusted to vote independently.

More crucially, the Levellers never managed to become a broad-based movement; they had support in London and in the army but their appeal never reached the vast majority of the population. With no clear organisation and no support among the senior officers (Colonel Rainborough was the most senior Leveller officer and his death in 1648 was crucial), they were doomed.

It would be true to say that although the Levellers as a coherent group no longer presented a threat to the Republic, or later to the Protectorate, Levellerism as an attitude of mind still lingered on. Some Levellers, such as Sexby and Wildman, continued to plot against the Protectorate, bizarrely in alliance with Royalist exiles, and perhaps posed a threat to Cromwell's life. More important was the memory of the heady days of 1647–8 that lingered on among some of the junior officers. They were to hanker after reform throughout the 1650s without a coherent set of ideas as to a programme.

The religious radicals

With the collapse of the authority of the Church of England in the run-up to the Civil War, many new, or previously underground, religious attitudes appeared. Unauthorised preaching both in and outside the army helped to spread them. By the late 1640s several strands of religious thought, outside of the Anglican, Presbyterian or Independent strands, can be seen.

Baptists. In the early 1650s **Baptists**, believing in adult baptism to produce a 'born-again' Christian, were numerically probably the largest sect. Opponents of Baptists tended to refer to them as Anabaptists. This was a reference to a rising in 1530 in Munster in Germany where a Baptist sect created a communist-style city state which degenerated rapidly into a dictatorship. Significantly, it was put down by local Catholic and Protestant princes, fearful of the social ideas involved. The strength of the Baptists was probably in the army. Fleetwood, Commander in Ireland and later in England, was a Baptist. He promoted Baptists and a significant group of army officers became Baptists. Despite the deep suspicion in which Baptists were held by the more orthodox

KEY THEME

Cromwell's attitude towards the Baptists

Cromwell tended to tolerate Baptists from the beginning of his career. In one of his classic statements about toleration, he wrote to a Presbyterian officer who had dismissed a Baptist: 'The man is an Anabaptist . . . admit he be, shall that render him incapable to serve the public? . . . Sir, the state, in choosing men to serve them, takes no notice of their opinions; if they be willing faithfully to serve them, that satisfies.'

Puritans it cannot be said that they constituted any kind of threat to the Protectorate.

The Fifth Monarchists. As already discussed, the Fifth Monarchists, with their belief in the imminent return of Christ and their desire to create His Kingdom on Earth before His arrival, were certainly a potent force behind the fall of the Rump in 1653. This was because, despite their small numbers, they had powerful backing from some army officers, principally Harrison. After the fall of the Barebones Parliament in December 1653, the Fifth Monarchists turned their anger on Cromwell who became, for them, 'the little horn of the great beast' of the book of Revelation in the Bible. However, they never constituted a real threat to the Protectorate because of their small numbers and loss of influence in the army with the departure of Harrison.

The other extreme sects. The Muggletonians claimed that their leader, Lodowick Muggleton, had been visited by Jesus Christ and had been given the power to say who was damned and who was saved. The Seekers and the Ranters were vague groups who had no real organisation, just claiming to be led by the Spirit of God. Muggletonians, Seekers and Ranters were all regarded with deep suspicion by most of the conventionally religious but they never attracted a wide following or created a proper organisation to challenge Interregnum governments.

The Quakers. In the 1650s, especially after 1653, the Quakers were seen as the most potent threat from a religiously radical standpoint. They rejected all authority and were seen as potentially violently subversive. As with the other radical sects, many were called 'Quakers' who held any view in common with them, so many solitary religious extremists were called 'Quakers' who probably were not. The religious maniac Naylor, who imitated Christ's entry into Jerusalem in 1657 by riding into Bristol on a donkey, was called a Quaker. The appalling punishments inflicted on him by the Second Protectorate Parliament were a measure of the fear and loathing that Quakerism aroused among the gentry. Characteristically, Cromwell, with his religious toleration, opposed the punishment of Naylor.

Certainly the Quakers were regarded as being a very dangerous group that was rapidly gaining adherents in the period 1655–9, but whether or not they constituted an organised danger to the Republic remains doubtful.

HOW SUCCESSFUL WAS CROMWELL'S FOREIGN POLICY?

Key themes

The main attacks on Cromwell's foreign policy have centred on three issues:

- Given the size of public debt, an active foreign policy only made the problem worse. Keeping a fleet of up to 150 vessels at sea, attacks on Spanish possessions in the Caribbean and support of France in Europe made the financial problems of the Protectorate far worse. Certainly, Cromwell would have been wiser, in purely financial terms, to have pursued a neutral foreign policy in the 1650s.
- However, that might not have been an option open to him, even if he could have restrained his strong views of England's destiny as a leading Protestant power.
- Cromwell undoubtedly had the idea that the English were God's chosen people and that their destiny was to lead Protestantism against the forces of **Antichrist**. This world-view did shape his foreign policy but there were practical considerations behind some of his moves.

KEY TERM

Antichrist The Devil, or the forces that opposed Christ and true Christianity.

The reduction of the Royalist threat from abroad. More than anything else it was important to deny Royalist exiles centred around Charles II safe havens, men and arms. With hindsight it can be seen that the exiles had very little real power to do the Protectorate (or, for that matter, the Rump) damage, but it did not seem that way at the time. Peace with the Dutch, alliance with France, all reduced the number of safe havens for exiled Royalists. By 1658 Charles II only had the very limited support of Spain and, even if Spanish troops could have been forthcoming for a Royalist invasion of England, the general hatred of Spain would probably have united the country against Charles II.

The end of the Dutch War. Slingsby Bethel asserted in *The World's Mistake in Oliver Cromwell* that Cromwell threw away a golden opportunity to destroy Dutch power and create the conditions favourable to English domination of trade. If that assertion is correct, then peace with the United Provinces on the terms of the Treaty of Westminster was an error. However, because English trade had become dominant by the nineteenth century and the English had captured the world's 'carrying trade' (by 1820, 70 per cent of the world's shipping was British), historians have tended to agree with Bethel. We could have destroyed the Dutch earlier – only Cromwell's Protestant attitudes prevented the inevitable. It may be so, but on the other hand two more Dutch wars had to be fought and even then Amsterdam did not really decline until the late seventeeth century. It is by no means certain that the English could have completely crushed the Dutch.

Even if a devastated United Provinces, bankrupt and defenceless, might have been the result of Cromwell's continuing the war, such a result could have ensured that either Spain, or later France, swallowed up the United Provinces. This would not, strategically, have been in England's interests. In the short term, a harsh peace with the Provinces might have brought back the Orangist/Stuart group to power.

The Spanish War. Cromwell's pursuit of the 'Western Design' is criticised in two ways:

- Firstly, it showed his out-of-date 'Elizabethan' attitude to foreign affairs – a Protestant crusade against the traditional enemy.
- Secondly, Spain was a declining power. France was the threat in the future and Cromwell should have supported Spain to maintain a balance of power in Europe.

On the first point of the 'Protestant Crusade', it is perfectly true that, to Cromwell, Spain was England's deadly enemy and he retained the attitudes of the average Protestant English country gentleman towards Spain. He ignored the fact that Spain had been anxious to open lines of communication to the Rump, even given its regicide nature. This showed that, in the last analysis, ideology and religion were less important in relations between European states by 1650 than power politics. In that respect it would be correct to say that Cromwell was living in the past.

On the issue of 'balance and power', much of the argument against the Spanish War is with hindsight. In the 1650s Spain still seemed a formidable power with a huge army and navy. It had suffered severe reverses in the Thirty Years War but was by no means finished.

The creation of the British Empire. It has been suggested that Cromwell's acquisition of Jamaica led the way to a colonial policy and founded the British Empire. Again, it can be argued that this is said with hindsight. The original target of Venables' attack had been Hispaniola (Haiti), to be used as a base to prey on Spanish treasure fleets – an extension of the Elizabethan sea war.

Cromwell's foreign policy was a success in that it gained a toehold in Europe (Dunkirk), a toehold in the Caribbean (Jamaica) and it secured the Protectorate against Royalist exiles. It was expensive, and inconclusive in other ways, possibly marginally assisting France towards a more dominant position in Europe. But it was out of date in a Europe where foreign policies based on religious considerations were being abandoned.

KEY THEME

Cromwell's foreign policy
Cromwell's policy can be compared with the status of England and the English navy under Charles I, and again under Charles II. When George Downing, who had served the Protectorate as an ambassador, complained about being kept waiting at the French Court in 1663, he was told: 'But under Cromwell you were a great power.'

Conclusion

Cromwell's greatness in foreign policy was to show England's potential to the world:

- **Navy.** Cromwell built a highly efficient navy that had blockaded the Spanish coast for nearly two years and which no Spanish fleet could face.
- **Army.** He also built an incomparable army which their French allies at the Battle of Dunes thought the strongest they had ever seen.

Clarendon wrote about Cromwell: 'His greatness at home was but a shadow of the glory he had abroad. It was hard to discover which feared him the most, France, Spain or the Low Countries.'

WHAT WAS THE ROLE OF THE ARMY IN THE 1650s?

Key themes

- Although the army represented security against anarchy and/or a Royalist Restoration, it was also the biggest single stumbling block to any settlement acceptable to the traditional political nation.
- Without the army, England would probably have experienced more civil wars, more upheaval. It had the power to keep all those opposed to the regimes of the Interregnum under control. The first standing army in English history, it could prevent uprisings and keep the lid on discontented Royalists and conservatives.

This very power and control was a source of constant friction. The republican Commonwealth Rumpers resented the army as a potential rival to their power. The traditional country gentry, used to exercising control over their localities, resented the existence of the army with its 'low-born' officers: 'tinkers, button makers and dunghill operators', as that arch conservative Lord Clarendon described them.

The cost of the army

It was not just the threat to the power of the gentry that was an issue, it was also the cost of the army – a cost that was to hobble successive regimes in the 1650s. The gentry wanted cheap government, low taxes and no interference from 'the centre'. The army ran straight across these aspirations. They not only provided a check on the influence and power of the gentry, they assured that taxation remained at a much higher level than during Personal Rule. Therefore, for the traditional political nation they were an object of resentment and suspicion.

The 'Good Old Cause'

This rather vague phrase was used throughout the 1650s by republicans, radicals and the army to describe what the Civil War had been fought for.

- To republicans and their allies, the Civil War had been fought to destroy absolutist monarchy, to establish government by 'the people' and to institute reform. Who constituted 'the people' and what 'reform' should take place remained issues.
- For the army, *they* were the embodiment of the 'Good Old Cause', standing between republican governments and a possible Stuart Restoration, and supporting the aims of those who had ideals such as religious toleration, law reform and even political reform. Not many of the gentry could be said to be sympathetic to the 'Good Old Cause'.

While the army existed, with its suspect political and religious ideals, challenging the 'traditional' rules of the countryside and parliaments, any really lasting, durable settlement was difficult.

The role of the army in politics in the 1650s

The army was not an entirely united organisation. The various factions were held together by their determination to resist a Stuart Restoration, their belief in religious toleration and their desire to ensure that the gentry in Parliament were never in a position to dispense with their services. This was the 'lowest common denominator'. More senior officers wished to ensure that the **army remained politically influential** by having direct means of putting pressure on parliaments.

This pattern was to continue in both Protectorate parliaments. The Council of the Protectorate had no fewer than seven senior officers' names in the Instrument of Government. These senior officers had an interest in the continuation of their posts and therefore in the continued existence of a large army. The Instrument of Government had ensured this, although the size of the army, laid down by the Instrument, was smaller than the actual army of December 1653. The senior officers would resist any attacks on the army by gentry politicians wishing to cut down, or disband it.

What was the army's attitude towards religion? In religion the army, believing in religious toleration, was a mixture. There were Presbyterians, such as Monck, Baptists, such as Fleetwood, religious radicals or 'sectaries', such as Goffe, but the majority of the officers, junior and senior, tended to be Independents of various degrees of radicalism. There were even some Quakers. More orthodox officers, such as Monck, clamped down on them.

KEY THEME

Soldiers in Parliament Senior army officers sat in the Barebones Parliament and in both Protectorate parliaments. Generals Fleetwood, Monck (at that time attached to the navy), Lambert, Harrison and Desborough and Colonels Clark and Hewson all sat in the Barebones Parliament.

What were the political divisions within the army? In politics there were far more serious *potential* divides. Leveller ideas still seemed to be loosely held by the more junior officers, while their seniors were more conservative. For most of the time these were merely undercurrents of disagreement, but in April 1659 Sir Arthur Heselrige was able to drive a wedge between the senior officers and the junior officers by promising the latter that a restored Rump would listen sympathetically to their ideas of reform. What is amazing, given his track record from 1650–3, is that the junior officers believed him. Until the drift towards anarchy in 1659–60, these divisions within the army should not be overestimated. The army had more to unite it than divide it.

Cromwell, the army and settlement

As discussed, Cromwell's control over this politicised yet professional army was one of the keys to his dominance of the 1650s. He knew its personnel, its inner tensions and rivalries and, most important of all, he was able to keep the trust of the majority of the army, even when he seemed, after 1653, to be moving in a more conservative direction, making bridges to the country gentry. His biggest mistake in looking for settlement was probably the Major Generals experiment of 1655–6, which the country gentry generally hated. However, Cromwell was able to abandon both it and the influence that the army enjoyed during the experiment without an army revolt.

Even the Humble Petition and Advice of 1657, which caused disquiet among many of the officers, did not lead to an army revolt. Lambert, charismatic though he was, was sent into retirement (although with a large pension) and Colonel Packer and five captains were dismissed. The rest of the army remained puzzled, possibly resentful, but reluctant to revolt against their leader who had led them to their remarkable series of victories. Cromwell seems to have had a hold over their imaginations and their loyalty that was proof against all the twists and turns of his policies in the 1650s. There were limits – the army could not abandon the 'Good Old Cause' and accept Cromwell's taking the Crown.

Despite this limitation, Cromwell's control over the army was secure. While he lived, the army would hold together and be controlled. Cromwell moved slowly towards his goal of cutting down the size of the army to a level that would be acceptable in terms of the tax burden, while supporting his loyal comrades who had, as an old soldier wrote to him, 'followed him from Edgehill to Dunbar'.

The effect of the death of Oliver Cromwell on army politics. Just before Cromwell died on 3 December 1658 he was preparing another purge of the army to ensure a smooth succession for his son Richard. Had he completed this 'purge', the history of Richard's Protectorate might have been quite different. It can be argued that, had the army been properly brought under control in the last months of Oliver's life, the Protectorate could have survived.

Richard or Henry?

Richard's inability to act quickly and decisively, despite Monck's advice to move against his army enemies, has prompted speculation that had Oliver chosen another son, Henry, as Lord Protector then the Protectorate could have survived. **Henry Cromwell** had successfully controlled ambitious trouble-making politicians in Ireland. He had also pleased the Anglo-Irish gentry. He might have done the same in England. However, the appointment of such a ruthless, decisive son of Cromwell might have triggered an army revolt before he could arrive from Ireland. The army politicians 'tolerated' Richard as a potentially weak Protector whom they could dominate (see Part 3).

To avoid a split in the spring of 1659, the army politicians abandoned Richard as he was an object of suspicion to the junior officers. For the more radical junior officers, encouraged by Heselrige, who wanted power back in the hands of the Commonwealth's-men, Richard was a 'conservative' prepared even to bring back Royalism. The 'Good Old Cause' demanded his fall. With Richard's fall, the stage was set for the confused events of the summer and autumn of 1659 that led to the Restoration of Charles II. There was, however, nothing inevitable about the eventual Restoration.

KEY PERSON

Henry Cromwell
Henry was Oliver Cromwell's fourth son. He was a military man who fought in Ireland in 1650. In 1655 he effectively became Ireland's ruler. Henry took little interest in English affairs and supported his brother Richard.

ASSESSMENT: THE ENGLISH REPUBLIC, 1649–60

SOURCES QUESTIONS IN THE STYLE OF OCR (A2)

The debate on Oliver Cromwell's ambition

Reading

Before answering the questions below you should read Chapters 7 and 8.

Read through the sources below and then answer the following questions.

Source A

(A Republican opponent of Cromwell attacks his ambition.)

Having seen our cause betrayed and the most solemn promises violated, I departed from my native county. General Cromwell had long been suspected by wise and good men; but he had taken such care to mould the army to his interests that he had filled all the places either with his own creatures or with such as hoped to share with him in the sovereignty, and removed those who had the courage to oppose him. His wicked intentions were not revealed open till after the battle at Worcester. Mr Hugh Peters said to a friend that Cromwell would make himself King. But either the General's ambition was so great that he could not resist ascending the throne until the time set by Parliament for its sitting had expired or his fear hastened him to the achievement of his plans. It is certain that he vehemently desired to be rid of this Parliament that had performed such great things.

Edmund Ludlow, *Memoirs*, 1698.

Source B

(An historian examines Cromwell's conflicting loyalties. Christopher Hill is a Marxist.)

His unique prestige with the Army made him the indispensable head of state so long as the army was a power in the land; his genuine desire for a parliamentary settlement continually raised hopes that he might yet square the circle. But, just because Oliver owed his position to the army, he could never in the last resort break from it. Oliver could ride the two horses, like a trick rider at the circus, though he could never transfer his weight from one to the other, and transform military rule into parliamentary government.

Christopher Hill, *Oliver Cromwell*, 1957.

Source C
(An historian evaluates Cromwell's ambition.)

I wrote this short account of Cromwell in 1939. The present version is revised. Yet the personality of Cromwell remains enigmatic and his reputation changes – as it will continue to change – with the moral and political climate of the living world. In 1939 the shadow of the European dictatorships darkened his image. The atmosphere has changed. He is generally recognised as a great figure in our history. But his career and character remain controversial. His actions in crisis, whether on the battlefield, in Parliament or at the Council table, show a clear and bold judgement; but he was not good at analysing or presenting the reasons behind his actions.

Prayer helped him towards all his considered decisions. In his years of power there is no evidence of any personal pleasure at his own greatness. Can this be taken as evidence that personal ambition was never a motive with him? I am inclined to think so. As Protector he appeared, in spite of his power at home and prestige abroad, a sad and heavily burdened man.

C V Wedgwood, *Oliver Cromwell*, 1973.

Source D
(An historian discusses Cromwell's 'dilemma'.)

The barren record of his first parliament made clear the dilemma which he faced as ruler of Britain. He had failed to give the people 'what pleases them' by constitutional means. His reaction was to embark on an authoritarian course of 'giving the people what's good for them'. Indeed many aspects of Cromwell's rule in 1655–56 show a lack of concern for constitutional legality that gives support to those who would depict Cromwell as a military dictator. Moreover, he underwent a personal, spiritual crisis in that period which caused him to be more than ever determined to take England, via the rule of the major-generals, into the New Jerusalem. Yet, what is striking about Cromwell, is that, even when his iron-fisted authoritarianism was most prominent, he showed those aspirations to secure broad-based support for his regime from the parliamentary classes of the country.

Barry Coward, *Oliver Cromwell*, 1991.

1a How effective is Source C in dealing with the accusation of ambition made against Cromwell in Source A? (15)

How to answer this question

The question is centred on a comparison of the two sources. To answer the question well you need to do the following:

- You must make use of both sources and ensure that you draw real comparisons between the two.
- You need to point out how the source is effective but also where it is less so.
- Use your own knowledge to back up your conclusions.
- Evaluate the sources by commenting where appropriate on their value, utility and reliability.

Content

Before you start writing you should try to identify how the sources agree and how they disagree. While Source A attacks Cromwell for his naked ambition, Source C attempts to come to a more balanced conclusion. This can be explained in a number of ways:

- One has to challenge Ludlow's motives for attacking Cromwell in this way. The reliability of his opinion is questionable given his opposition to Cromwell.
- The historian in Source C attempts to take a more subjective view. Her ideas have been revised and she recognises that the context in which she writes will affect her judgement.
- The argument of the author in Source C is somewhat generalised. This means that its effectiveness in dealing with the specific charges made in Source A is reduced; e.g. that Cromwell had packed the army with his own supporters.

Style

You should try to be as direct as possible when answering the question. Below are a couple of sentences from an answer. The candidate is pointing out the ways in which Source C is effective. Note that the candidate has attempted to focus directly on the question set.

The effectiveness of Source C is increased by the fact that Wedgwood attempts to come to some sort of balanced judgement about Cromwell recognising that whilst on the one hand he showed 'clear and bold judgement' on the other hand he was weak at 'analysing or presenting the reasons behind his actions'. This contrasts to the dismissive Ludlow who is an obvious opponent of Cromwell and only very one sided in his judgement, dismissing Cromwell's intentions with the emotive term 'wicked'.

1b What do Sources A to D tell us about the dilemma Cromwell faced as ruler of England? (30)

How to answer this question

To be marked at the higher levels of the mark scheme you need to do the following:

- Refer to all four sources. You must interpret each source, i.e. what does it say that will help you deal with the question, evaluate it and compare it against your own knowledge.
- You must try to show that you understand the dilemma that Cromwell faced.
- It is essential to plan your answer. Try to avoid dealing with the sources in alphabetical order. In your plan you should be able to look at the answer thematically. In the case of this question that means looking at the different problems.

Style

Below is an extract from an answer to this question. Note how the candidate has taken the sources as a set and is looking at the wider context of Cromwell's problems.

Perhaps the most pressing dilemma Cromwell faced was the choice between military and parliamentary government. This is well explained in Source D which gives a balanced and objective account of Cromwell's position. The source explains that on the one hand he wished to win support from 'the Parliamentary classes' whilst on the other hand his instincts as a soldier were to rule with 'iron fisted' authoritarianism. This contradiction was shown many times from the dissolution of Parliament in January 1655 to the Humble Petition and Advice 1657 which attempted to balance the constitution.

Whereas Source D attempts a balanced approach, Source A does not. It also recognises Cromwell's constitutional problem but does not portray the Protector as having a dilemma. Instead it paints him as an authoritarian wishing to 'be rid of this Parliament'. Whilst that was certainly Cromwell's aim at times it was not consistently so. We have to be wary of using Ludlow as evidence about Cromwell's intentions. His personal grudge and differences of opinion very much affect the objectivity of the evidence.

SOURCES QUESTIONS IN THE STYLE OF AQA (A2)

Oliver Cromwell and the Crown

Reading

For help in answering this assignment you should read Chapter 8 in this book.

Read the following sources and then answer the questions.

Source A
(*A conversation in 1651 between Hermann Mylius, envoy of Oldebury, and John Drury, librarian at St James' Palace.*)

[Drury:] Things will shortly happen which have been unheard of, and above all would open the eyes of those who live under the kings and other sovereigns, and lead to great changes. General Cromwell's prudence, gallantry and good fortune prevail.

[Mylius:] Perhaps they will make him a Doge in the Commonwealth, like the Venetians . . . and confer that dignity on him by hereditary right to continue in his descendants.

[Drury:] On this he cannot verify anything definite. [Cromwell] alone holds the direction of political and military affairs in his hands. He is one who is worth all the offers put together, and, in effect, King.

D L Smith, *Oliver Cromwell, Politics and Religion*, 1991

Source B
(*From Franceso Giavarina, Venetian ambassador in England, to the Doge and Senate, 6 April 1657.*)

They (Parliament) propose to go to Whitehall and offer him the crown . . . They are sure to perform this duty in a most submissive manner as if the Lord Protector was granting them a favour in accepting what he longed to have. Cromwell is certain to display his customary astuteness and profess his inability to support so great a burden . . . His assent is beyond all question since it has long been known that he aspired to the title and it is asserted that the crown is almost ready which is to serve for his coronation.

Source C
A rational explanation of Cromwell's refusal of the crown would assume that he feared the spread of disaffection through the army and the sects . . . Yet . . . Cromwell may have rejected the title for less rational reasons. He was distressed by allegations that he had worked for his own family's [increase in wealth and importance], and that in restoring monarchy he would be disobeying God's commands . . . Cromwell tended to dismiss the authority of the King as inconsequential, 'a gaudy feather in the hat of authority'.

T Barnard, *The English Republic 1649–69*, 1982.

1 Consult Source B. How valid is Giavarina's interpretation of Cromwell's attitude to the offer of the Crown? (10)

How to answer this question

You are to answer this question by doing the following:

- Discuss the validity of the comment throughout the answer.
- Test the validity of the answer by using your own knowledge.
- Come to a conclusion before you begin about the source's validity.

Style

Below is an extract from an answer to this question.

> The source's validity should be questioned in the light of Cromwell's subsequent rejection of the Crown. Whilst it is difficult to judge Cromwell's intentions regarding the Crown, this evidence tends too much to the view of Cromwell's enemies. The ambassador claims that Cromwell 'aspired to the title', a view which reflected the criticisms levelled at Cromwell by his enemies such as Ludlow and Lilburne.

2 Consult Source C. How useful is Source C in explaining Cromwell's rejection of the Crown in 1657? (10)

How to answer this question

Before answering questions about utility you need to take account of the following points:

- Compare the source's positive points, its limitations and also its reliability. You must also compare the usefulness of the source against your own knowledge.
- You are expected to mention the extent to which the author's views were typical of the period. Another question you should ask is what gaps there are in the evidence?
- The usefulness of a source depends on the questions asked of it. An example of such a question might be: 'Can it be corroborated (backed up) with other evidence?'

3 Use Sources A, B and C and your own knowledge.
'Cromwell alone holds the direction of political and military affairs in his hands.'
How far do you agree with this interpretation of the power of Oliver Cromwell in the period 1651–8? (20)

How to answer this question

In answering this question it is important that you select evidence from all the sources and make a judgement that you follow throughout.

Content

In answering this question you should use the following information from the sources:

- Source A discusses Cromwell's 'prudence' and 'gallantry'.
- Source B mentions his 'customary astuteness' and his political power in how he is able to manipulate Parliament.
- Source C discusses Cromwell's strength in being able to reject the Crown and his dismissive attitude to what he believed to be 'a gaudy feather in the hat of authority'.

From your own knowledge you should discuss Cromwell's attitudes towards Parliament and foreign policy, his control of the army and his role as Lord Protector, and the offer of the Crown.

ESSAY QUESTION IN THE STYLE OF OCR (AS)

1 How valid is the judgement that Cromwell was 'the lost leader of the English Revolution'? (45)

How to answer this question

Before you start writing you should study the question carefully. There are two important points to note:

- By 'lost leader' the question suggests that Cromwell betrayed many of the political and religious ideals he had championed during the Civil War.
- The idea of the 'English Revolution' is an issue which will need to be addressed.

Then you have to decide the extent to which you agree with the validity of the statement.

Content

In answering the question you might deal with the following areas:

- Cromwell's attitude towards Parliament, the nature of his rule, how he dealt with the different sects and radical groups, the issue of religious toleration.

PART 3: THE RESTORATION

INTRODUCTION

The Restoration

When Richard Cromwell succeeded his father as Lord Protector in 1658, in some ways he seemed in a strong position. The army were suspicious of him, but the traditional country gentry were more supportive. He failed, however, to deal swiftly and ruthlessly with the ambitious politicians in the army who threatened his position, with the result that his Parliament was dissolved and he was ousted in April 1659. Fifty members of the old Rump Parliament returned to Westminster.

The army and the Rump soon fell out, however, and in the autumn of 1659 the army politicians established a form of military dictatorship – an emergency government called the Committee of Safety. The public by this time was totally disillusioned and the Committee had no support. Since the public debt was running at a very high level, the ordinary soldiers were unpaid and the army lost faith in their senior officers and the Committee.

General Monck, in Scotland, saw England sinking into anarchy and forced the restoration of the Rump, in December 1659. He then marched south with his loyal army to restore order and support the civilian politicians. He soon came to realise that the Rump was as unpopular as the Committee of Safety and only a return to the 'old constitution' with a king at its head was going to bring stability. He therefore engineered the end of the Rump and the calling of a Parliament that opened negotiations with Charles II, in exile in Holland. In May 1660 Charles II was restored.

AS: NARRATIVE AND EXPLANATION

CHAPTER 10

From Richard Cromwell to the Restoration

THE PROTECTORATE OF RICHARD CROMWELL, SEPTEMBER 1658–APRIL 1659

Richard's advantages
- Richard Cromwell was generally welcomed by the gentry and the merchant classes.
- He received 196 addresses of welcome and loyalty from gentry, counties and town corporations.
- Richard was acceptable to the traditional political nation because he was not associated with the death of the King in any way, nor with the Civil Wars.
- He had a pleasant manner, and had a wide group of gentry friends including Royalists.

Richard's disadvantages
These very qualities made him an object of suspicion to the army. He had few contacts in it and to many in the army he seemed a weak country squire.

Attitudes of the senior officers. The senior officers stationed in London were determined to extend their political influence from the beginning of Richard's Protectorate. They met at **Wallingford House** to coordinate their tactics.

As soon as he took office, Richard received good advice from General Monck, a Cromwellian loyalist who commanded the army in Scotland.

- He advised Richard to cut down the size of the army immediately, by putting two regiments into one.

KEY THEME

The Wallingford House 'Party' would only accept Richard's Protectorship if he put the interests of the army first. The senior army officers had no love for the Protectorate as a form of government.

Richard Cromwell.

- He pointed out that a quick purge would have two advantages; it would remove officers who were disloyal to the Protectorate, and it would reduce the crippling public debt.

Richard did not have the courage to take Monck's advice.

Richard Cromwell's Parliament, January–April 1659

The Council made a curious unexplained decision to go back to the old pre-Instrument of Government system of voting for elections to Richard's Parliament which met on 27 January 1659. In some ways, the Parliament was a 'rerun' of Oliver's Parliaments – little was achieved.

- The Commonwealth's-men, again led by Heselrige and Vane, attacked the whole constitutional legality of the Protectorate.
- On the other side, the conservatives were determined to control the army. By April 1659 they were planning a motion that would put control of the army completely in the hands of Richard, the Upper House and the House of Commons. The senior officers' promotions and actions would therefore be completely controlled by civilians.

Potential splits in the army. Meanwhile, Heselrige had been stirring up the junior officers, arguing that, if the Protectorate was abolished and the present Parliament removed, the Rump could be restored. This restored Rump, he suggested, would now be prepared to listen to demands for reform which the more radical junior officers still hoped for. The senior officers began to fear a split in the army between themselves (who some junior officers saw as well-paid comfortable men who had abandoned their principles) and the more radical juniors, short of pay and republican-minded. To avoid this split Fleetwood and Lambert (who was waiting for the moment to be reinstated in his command) decided to throw Richard out of office and dissolve the Parliament that seemed to threaten their position.

The fall of Richard

On 21 April 1659 Richard called a rendezvous of troops loyal to him, to protect him and the Parliament. Their commander Ingoldsby found the troops melting away when faced with regiments loyal to the Wallingford House Party, aided by the inspiring presence of Lambert who had great status with the ordinary soldiers. On 22 April Parliament was dissolved and, on 7 May, 50 members of the old Rump took their seats at Westminster. Richard was never formally deposed but merely retired and the Protectorate just died.

THE COMMONWEALTH RE-ESTABLISHED

The failure of the Rump, May–October 1659

The restored Rump faced the same problems as all the previous governments:

- public debt,
- unpopularity,
- the lurking threat of army politicians.

Heselrige and his colleagues were quite incapable of dealing with these problems. They represented such a small group of gentry republicans that they could not hope to get support from the rest of the political nation. They did

KEY THEME

Heselrige's lack of reality
Sir Arthur Heselrige was a Puritan and a strong supporter of Pym and then Cromwell. However, after the Rump was expelled, Heselrige became an opponent of Cromwell. In 1659 he had a brief return to authority with the return of the Rump.

In the summer of 1659 a conversation with Lambert took place that illustrates Heselrige's lack of reality: 'You are only at the mercy of Parliament who are your good friends', he told Lambert. Lambert's reply was: 'I do not see why you should not be at ours.' The threat was not grasped by Heselrige.

nothing to deal with the problems of public finance. Their relations with the army quickly grew worse. Once back in power, Heselrige dropped his friendship with the radical junior officers, having no intention of bringing in the reforms they hoped for.

Heselrige treated the senior officers almost with contempt. He never gave the impression that he would consider their demands for control over promotions and did not appear to understand the power of the army.

Booth's Rebellion, July 1659

The truce of the spring and early summer of 1659 was ended by a potentially dangerous uprising in Cheshire which broke out on 31 July. The rebellion was led by Sir George Booth, a Presbyterian who had fought for Parliament in the First Civil War. His rallying call was for a 'Free Parliament' – new elections. Such elections might well produce a Royalist House of Commons, given how disillusioned the country was with the Rump. In effect, Booth's Rebellion was an attempt to restore Charles II. Lambert marched north, **defeating Booth** easily at Winnington Bridge on 18 August.

The failure of Booth's Rebellion

- Despite the unpopularity of the Rump the public gave Booth little support. The local militia fought with Lambert, but the other risings planned to coincide with Booth's did not happen. It can be concluded that, whatever the views of the political nation, another civil war was not a price anyone was prepared to pay to restore Charles II.
- Many Royalists refused to support Booth because he was a Presbyterian not an Anglican, and because of his former Parliamentarian military career. Thus the forces opposed to the Republic were as divided as ever.

The effects of Booth's Rebellion

- It strengthened the position of the army against the Rump. The army could now claim that without them the Rump would have been overthrown and therefore the Rump needed the army.

KEY EVENT

Booth's capture. Sir George, perhaps not the most competent conspirator, escaped disguised as a woman, but was captured after asking an innkeeper for a shave.

- Fleetwood and Lambert chose this opportunity to call for extra regiments from Ireland. These regiments were commanded by army politicians such as Colonel Sankey who was an ally of Fleetwood.
- The immediate result of the defeat of Booth was the **Derby Petition** drawn up by the army in September 1659, inspired by the likes of Sankey with the encouragement of Fleetwood and Lambert.

KEY THEME

The Derby Petition, September 1659 The Petition demanded a political settlement acceptable to the army, and army control over promotions. The Rump condemned it, Heselrige even suggesting that Lambert should be sent to the Tower. Sir Arthur again appeared not to realise the power that Lambert had.

The Rump's attempt to control the army and the fall of the Rump

In October the army continued to put pressure on the Rump and on 12 October the Rump tried to reassert control over the army by dismissing nine officers, including Lambert. At the same time, like Richard before them, they attempted to organise a defence of Parliament with regiments they thought would be loyal to them. On 13 October these again melted away at the approach of Lambert's troops, and the Rump was dispersed.

The Committee of Safety, October 1659

The senior officers had removed the Rump, but really had no idea what to put in its place. On 26 October a **Committee of Safety** was set up, composed of army officers and some civilian opportunists such as Sir Gilbert Pickering.

The drift to Restoration, winter 1659

By the time the Committee had been set up the situation was moving out of control:

- Public debt was over two million pounds.
- The public simply refused to accept the Committee as having any legal basis. It had no support in the country.
- The public went on a tax strike, refusing to pay taxes to an illegal regime.
- The army itself was becoming demoralised – it was unpaid, living at 'free quarter'. The soldiers and junior officers became increasingly resentful of the senior officers and the loyalty of the army to Fleetwood and Lambert began to erode rapidly.
- There was an upsurge in radical political activity with Leveller pamphlets beginning to circulate again.

KEY TERM

Committee of Safety The Committee was a desperate measure of army politicians who could break governments but had no idea how to govern themselves. The senior officers were shown as unprincipled people interested only in power. They had really set up a military dictatorship.

- Radical religious groups were again seen as a threat – the Quakers were now the main bogeymen.
- Because of all these circumstances, the propertied classes became terrified of a complete breakdown in law and order.

The Committee of Safety was unable to control the situation. Apprentice riots in the city resulted in deaths when Colonel Hewson ordered his troops to open fire, while garrisons at Portsmouth and Hull, together with the fleet, refused to obey its orders.

General Monck

The events in England had been watched by **George Monck** in Scotland. He realised that England was on the verge of anarchy, and wrote to Fleetwood and Lambert urging them to restore civilian authority. Unlike Fleetwood and Lambert, he had a secure power base because his army, paid by Scottish taxes, and completely loyal to him, would follow his orders. Fleetwood exchanged letters with Monck during November 1659 trying, unsuccessfully, to justify the coup of October. Monck made it clear that unless civilian government, that is the Rump, was restored he would march south. Meanwhile, Lambert moved north to face the threat that Monck posed.

The break-up of the army in England. Disillusion had set in among Lambert's troops: 'We will make a ring for our officers to fight in', was how a pamphlet put it. Monck managed to distribute skilful propaganda among Lambert's troops while preventing any of Lambert's propaganda reaching his. By mid-December Lambert's unpaid army had dissolved. Meanwhile, in the south, the Portsmouth garrison had declared for the Rump, as had the fleet, which blockaded the Thames. Lambert and Fleetwood had no option but to restore the Rump on 26 December.

Monck marches south. On 1 January 1660 Monck crossed the River Tweed into England and marched south, to support the restored Rump and end the threat of the army politicians once and for all. However, on his march south, Monck was presented with hundreds of petitions calling for a 'Free Parliament', in other words, a proper general election.

KEY THEME

Monck's character He genuinely believed that soldiers should obey the orders of civilian governments and, like Cromwell, he feared anarchy. Because he was a man of few words, the senior officers in England had always regarded him as slow and stupid and completely underestimated him. In fact he was a very shrewd politician.

General Monck.

- By now the public, although delighted at the fall of the hated army politicians, had no time for the discredited Rump either.
- Public opinion was united in a way almost never seen before, in wishing to get rid of the Rump and return to the old ways.
- The Rump, of course, had learnt nothing from its experiences. The Rumpers refused to set a date for new elections and imprisoned those who sent them petitions.

The fall of the Rump

Monck arrived in London on 3 February, in a wave of popularity. Heselrige was already suspicious of him – a popular soldier with a loyal army at his back was an obvious threat. Monck told the Rump in a speech on 6 February that he had received all those petitions for a 'Free Parliament', leaving a strong hint that the Rump should dissolve itself and allow new elections. The Rumpers had no intention of exposing themselves to public opinion in this way and his speech was, naturally, unpopular with them. Heselrige attempted to destroy Monck's popularity by ordering him to occupy the City of London to break the tax strike. Monck moved into the City on 11 February but, instead of oppressing the citizens, held discussions with groups opposed to the Rump, most importantly the excluded members: those who had been ejected from the Long Parliament by Pride's Purge in 1648.

The return of the excluded members. In exchange for a promise that they would, if allowed back into the House of Commons, set a date for the dissolution of Parliament and new 'free elections', he agreed to have them escorted back to the House of Commons on 21 February. As the 100 excluded members outnumbered the Rumpers by 50 or so, they could pass a vote for a dissolution and a new election – the republicans could not stop them. The dissolution of Parliament took place on 16 March 1660.

Monck's skill. It was obvious that, because of the chaos of the autumn and winter of 1659 and the unpopularity of the republican Rumpers, public opinion had swung in favour of Restoration.

- The prime mover had been Monck, who had skilfully concealed his intentions and taken public opinion with him.
- The Royalists had been slow to see the significance of Monck and he had been careful not to have contact with them. He gave nothing away in conversations with them – one Royalist described him as 'That dark man General Monck'.
- Indeed Royalist agents did not have any discussions with him until Sir John Grenville contacted him as late as 17 March.
- It was important that, given the number of people that might have cause to fear a restoration of Charles II and therefore start desperate uprisings, Monck proceeded very slowly and carefully.
- Monck could not, at this stage, let his own army know that he was moving towards restoring the King.

The Convention Parliament, April 1660

The Parliament that met on 25 April is known as the Convention Parliament because it was not called by the King. The question facing this Parliament was not whether Charles would be restored, but under what conditions. Some Presbyterians wanted to ensure that Charles accepted Presbyterianism as the state religion but they failed to force this through.

The Declaration of Breda. Meanwhile, Monck had been in communication with Charles II and Hyde, his chief adviser, at Breda. The result of this was the **Declaration of Breda** which had been drafted on 4 April. The Declaration was the last act before Restoration but it was important. It made it clear that Charles had no intention of ruling as an absolutist and that there would be no bloodbath of former Parliamentarians who had fought his father. Without this assurance many would have seen support for Restoration as suicide. As important was the promise to pay Monck's troops, or to take them into royal service. However loyal his troops were, Monck could not expect them to support their own unemployment or poverty, so the promise kept his army together in support of Restoration.

Charles is proclaimed King. Charles was proclaimed King on 8 May, and arrived at Dover on the 25th to scenes of great rejoicing – the diarist John Evelyn recorded, 'I stood in the Strand and beheld it and blessed God. And all this was done without a drop of blood shed, and by that very army that had rebelled against him.' Evelyn was right – the Restoration of Charles II owed little to the Royalists and nearly everything to Monck who commanded a section of the army that had fought Charles I and Charles II.

KEY THEME

The Declaration of Breda

• Free pardon to all those who had fought Charles I and Charles II – only Parliament could punish former enemies of the monarchy.
• Parliament to settle the problem of religion – the King was prepared to grant religious toleration.
• The question of Royalist land confiscated and sold to new owners to be settled by Parliament – the King would not interfere.
• The King would take the advice of Parliament.
• Monck's army would be paid their arrears of pay and be taken into a Royal army.

SUMMARY QUESTION

1 Explain the role Monck played in the restoration of the monarchy in 1660.

A2: ANALYSIS AND INTERPRETATION

SECTION 4

Why was Charles II restored in 1660?

Key themes
- The restoration of the monarchy was not inevitable. In 1658 the Protectorate was secure.
- The role of the army was crucial to the Restoration, both in its attitude to Richard and because of its own divisions.

The weaknesses of the opposition on the death of Oliver Cromwell. On the death of Oliver Cromwell, despite the Royalists' immediate rejoicing and hoping for a collapse, the regime seemed secure. Thurloe's reports to Henry Cromwell in Ireland, reports of probably the best-informed man in England, were that the country was quiet, 'not a dog stirs amongst us'. Royalists in England remained cautious; they had seen the failure of Penruddock's Rising of 1655, they had much to lose by a failed coup and the army remained united and formidable. Opponents on the 'left' of the regime, from Commonwealth's-men to religious and political radicals, had no organisation, no clear programme and no access to the levers of power. The Quakers had the ability to frighten the 'men of property', the conservative-minded, but they had no means of overthrowing the government.

Richard Cromwell as a compromise. Given that Richard Cromwell was regarded as a young man who had played no part in the upheavals of the 1640s and 1650s, that he had ex-Royalist friends such as Fauconberg, and seemed not to be touched by regicide or religious 'enthusiasm', his ability to build bridges to the traditional political nation were undoubted. Those who could never accept the regicide Oliver could accept his son and the addresses of loyalty from counties and corporation were genuine.

Those who yearned for the restoration of the Stuarts in the shape of Charles II had to accept that, with the existence of the army, such a restoration was only going to take place as the result of a bloody and risky fourth civil war. For many Royalists, then, acceptance of the Protectorate of Richard Cromwell was a safe 'second best'. Many Royalists had been fined, lost estates and suffered imprisonment in the past 13 years – a rising on behalf of Charles II was not an attractive proposition given the chances of failure. For the vast majority of the political nation the wars had been a traumatic experience not to be repeated. If Richard could provide stability, then another bloody upheaval could be avoided. Royalist agents from abroad confirmed, pessimistically, this analysis. No one was going to risk anything to restore Charles II.

KEY THEME

Richard's chances of survival The Venetian ambassador had noted in October 1658 that if Richard did not have control over the army his chances of survival were slim: 'the Protector who claims to have succeeded his father as generalissimo of all forces without which his other office is worth little or nothing'. He also noted that the senior officers were already plotting against Richard.

The importance of the army. However, **Richard's position** was not as strong as general public opinion would have indicated. He had few active supporters in the army in England. From the beginning the senior officers hoped to mould Richard to their will, while the junior officers regarded him with deep suspicion. Without Oliver's reputation with the army, or his intimate knowledge of its officers, Richard never had the control over the army that his father had.

The officers assembled at Wallingford House saw Richard as a convenience at best – if he would not do the army's will then his days were numbered. To many officers the whole idea of the Protectorate was only acceptable because the Protector had been Oliver Cromwell, and they had accepted it reluctantly. Probably the senior officers such as Fleetwood and Desborough were prepared to live with a Protectorate provided the interests of their group were safeguarded. The more junior officers were outright republicans: the Protectorate should go and then would come the opportunity for the 'Good Old Cause', republicanism, and radicalism would reassert itself.

Divisions in the army. The seeds of a split in the army can be discerned in these months. The senior officers were almost 'courtiers', staying in London while their juniors were running the regiments and garrisons, i.e. doing the work. The debenture market was in London; senior officers were trading in 'promise notes' on Irish land that had been used to pay troops. They purchased these debentures for far less than they were worth on paper, often at up to 80 per cent discount, and then resold them on the debenture market in London. The junior officers and troops were owed pay and had no choice but to accept what they could get for the promise notes but resentment at the senior officers filling their pockets smouldered to the surface.

The Protectorate Parliament, January–March 1659. The Parliament, called under the old 'forty shilling' freehold voting qualification, was in many ways a conservative one. The county gentry were opposed to the army and made it clear that they were. Significantly, there was a small group of Commonwealth's-men led by Heselrige who were determined to sabotage support for Richard. They had no success within Parliament but outside they were crucial. Heselrige and Vane had established contacts with the junior officers and left the impression that, if the Protectorate were abolished and the Rump restored, then their demands for reform would be met. The senior officers, whatever their view of Richard, dared not support him and split the army, so the Protectorate Parliament, and with it the Protectorate, fell, destroyed by the army and a few civilian allies.

Still Restoration was not a possibility. In theory the forces that destroyed Richard were those most *opposed* to Restoration – the republican army and the Commonwealth's-men.

However, the return of the Rump did not in any way ensure stable government. Heselrige blocked the army's ideas of reform and the Rump carried on in much the same way as it had in 1650–3, to the disillusionment of the army. Booth's Rebellion in the summer of 1659 showed how little enthusiasm there was for Restoration; the country still preferred almost any regime to renewed civil war.

It was when the forces opposed to Restoration finally fell out among themselves that, with hindsight, Restoration seemed possible.

The collapse into anarchy. The Derby Petition, the ousting of the Rump by the army and the Committee of Safety all marked milestones on the road to the collapse of public order. By December 1659 the tax strike, public disgust with self-seeking army politicians and their unprincipled civilian allies, such as Sir Gilbert Pickering, showed how far the situation had deteriorated since the summer.

How significant was the role of Monck? There is no doubt that Monck's intervention was crucial. His complete control over his army, his political skill at outmanoeuvring the restored Rumpers and his public popularity all came together to make him the crucial figure in the period January to March 1660. His decision to readmit the excluded members on 21 February was the major step to Restoration. Before that Monck had had to play a waiting game: waiting until Lambert's and Fleetwood's unpaid, demoralised army had dissolved, waiting for public opinion to support his intervention, and waiting until, inevitably, Heselrige and the Rumpers finally overreached themselves and lost the last vestige of public support.

Monck's skill was in this waiting game. He had already seen, on his march south in January 1660, how public opinion had swung in favour of a 'Free Parliament' and that such a 'Free Parliament' would probably open negotiations with Charles II as a symbol of stability. However, his own army was republican, although loyal to him, so he had to move slowly. He let Heselrige, Scot and Vane finally lose all credibility with the public and, as importantly, the City of London. He got guarantees from the excluded members before he readmitted them, and he was most careful to ensure that his contacts with Royalists were verbal. Some thought, in early 1660, that Monck could, with his popularity, make himself Lord Protector, but his ambitions were limited, unlike his political skill. He realised that, despite all the seeming obstacles, public opinion was for Restoration; only Restoration, with guarantees of payment for the army, religious toleration and no revenge on Charles's enemies, could settle the country.

The Royalists would accept Restoration on any terms. Monck had to ensure that former Parliamentarians, republicans, his army and other opponents of Restoration would be reassured. Despite the swing of public opinion in favour of Restoration, Monck wished to avoid uprisings by desperate republicans, and unrest in his own army. Thus Lambert's attempt at an army rendezvous, to oppose the tide towards Restoration in April 1660, was an ignominious failure. This was as much due to the bankruptcy of the republican cause as to Monck but, through January to April 1660, Monck can be seen as the architect of Restoration. **Ronald Hutton** likens his skill to 'a chess grandmaster'.

With the complete dissipation and demoralisation of those opposed to Restoration by the spring of 1660, and with public debt at an unsupportable level, Monck could open negotiations with Charles II as the only possible figure who could provide stability. It only needed the reassurances contained in the Declaration of Breda to prevent any final republican uprising, or counter-coup, to ensure the bloodless Restoration. The Royalists had little part to play in the Restoration; it was the result of George Monck's activities, public opinion, the final political failure of the forces of republicanism, and the break-up of the army that had overtly or covertly been such a force in English politics since 1648.

ASSESSMENT: THE RESTORATION

SOURCES QUESTIONS IN THE STYLE OF OCR (AS)

Reading
Before answering the questions below you should read Part 3.

The Restoration of Charles II
Read the sources and answer the questions which follow.

Source A
(*From Francesco Giavarina, Venetian ambassador in England, to the Dodge and Senate, 16 April 1660.*)

The change in the people here is indeed miraculous . . . The king's name is now as much loved, revered and acclaimed as in the past years it was detested and abused, and nothing is desired with greater fervour by all, particularly those of the lower classes, as well as one of the (capital) as of the rest of the country who have been the most bitter enemies of his Majesty, so that it will be a marvel to see the moment of his coming without the shedding of a single drop of blood . . . The desire for the king is universal, some upon rigorous conditions, some on moderate ones and some freely, referring everything to the clemency of his Majesty.

Source B
The complete transformation in the king's position owed everything immediately to Monk, and more generally to the reaction in public opinion in favour of the monarchy, and little or nothing to the royal ministers abroad or cavalier agents in Britain . . .

Hyde's main service in the months before the Convention met was to remain inactive . . . By avoiding premature commitment to any . . . form of settlement . . . he preserved the widest scope for manoeuvre on Charles' part . . . The keynote was struck by the Declaration of Breda, with a general appeal for unity.

J R Jones, *Country and Court*, 1978.

1a Study Sources A and B. Explain how the two sources show both similar and different attitudes to the restoration of the monarchy in 1660. (10)

How to answer this question

To gain top marks in answering this question you need to:

- Ensure that you select information from both sources.
- Use your own knowledge to help answer the question.

It is essential that you sustain a judgement throughout your answer. To do this you must decide before you start how similar and how different the sources are in relation to the issue in question; in this case attitudes towards the Restoration. Therefore, a plan is essential. In your plan you can draw up the lines of argument that make a sustained judgement possible.

Plan

Below is an example of the type of plan you might choose to draw up. Note that in the key points the candidate has tried to answer the question.

Key points

- The similarities between the sources are more apparent than the differences. Both sources stress the role of and change in popular opinion. They also highlight the absence of a settlement which made the Restoration easier because it minimised opposition.
- However, there are subtle differences which should not be dismissed. The differences in interpretation arise from when the sources were written and the aims of the authors. Source A lacks the hindsight of Source C and thereby ignores the role of Monk, the relative insignificance of the royalists and the significance of the Declaration of Breda.

You should then plan a running order for the points you are going to make.

1b Study both sources and use your knowledge. 'The desire for the king is universal.' How far was the restoration of the monarchy in 1660 due to political and social factors rather than to the actions of Charles II? (20)

How to answer this question

Before answering this question you need to plan your answer.

Before you start you need to make sure that you understand the demands of the question. There are essentially two kinds of questions you will be asked:

- One kind of question asks you to look at the reason for an event.

- The other kind of question demands that you weigh up the relative importance of the question. Therefore the answer is often 'up to a point . . . but/to a certain extent . . . but'.

In this case the question asks you to weigh up the importance of political and social factors as against the importance of the actions of Charles II.

Your answer needs to include evidence from the two sources. It also needs to include evidence from your own knowledge.

You must sustain a judgement throughout your answer. This you do through planning.

Plan

Here are a couple of key points which are examples of the type of points you might put in your plan.

- The Restoration of Charles II was to a considerable extent due to political and social factors, in particular the role of Monk and popular opinion and especially the dislike of the military and the Rump.
- However, Charles did play an important role in the Restoration, in particular in not making demands of Parliament which would have prevented his return.

Style

Below is an extract from an answer to this question. Please note that the candidate has answered in a direct manner.

Political factors are the most important reason why the Restoration took place. Of these political factors Monck's intervention was crucial. His complete control over his army, his political skill at outmanoeuvring the restored Rumpers and his public popularity, all came together to make him the crucial figure in the period January to March 1660. His decision to readmit the excluded members on the 21 February was the major step to Restoration. Before that Monck had had to play a waiting game: waiting until Lambert and Fleetwood's unpaid, demoralised army had dissolved, waiting for public opinion to support his intervention, waiting until, inevitably, Hesilrige and the Rumpers finally over reached themselves and lost public support. Monck's skill was in this waiting game. He had already seen, on his march south in January 1660, how public opinion had swung in favour of a "Free Parliament" and that such a "Free Parliament" would probably open negotiations with Charles II as a symbol of stability.

DOCUMENTS SECTION

Below are three documents relevant to the Restoration. The aim behind the following exercise is to help you develop the skills necessary to tackle documents questions.

Read the sources and then answer the questions which follow.

Source A
(*General Monck's Declaration, December 1659.*)

Having a call from God and his people to march into England, to assert and maintain the liberty and being of parliament, our ancient constitution, and therein the freedom and rights of the people of these three nations from arbitrary and tyrannical usurpations upon their consciences, persons, and estates.

Source B
(*The Diary of Thomas Rugg (a city merchant), November 1659.*)

Then on the fifth day of December the apprentices and other discontented young men did, as well as [they] could, gather themselves together, for that over night they had contrived a rising in the morning, if possible; for they were now quite weary of the soldiery, which they knew well enough. In the morning the apprentices began to appear in a disorderly manner, but with a foot-ball, thinking that there would appear a party in arms for them; . . . Now the Committee of Safety, having intelligence that in London they had a great mind to be rid of the soldiery, they ordered that some regiments of horse and foot should forthwith march into the City, which accordingly they did, of horse and foot three thousand . . . Now there were many affronts offered and a great many of uncivil actions offered to them in their march into the City, but especially to Colonel Hewson's regiment of foot; they were more abused than any other. He was a cobbler by his trade, but a very stout man and a very good commander of foot; but in regard of his former employment and [what] the apprentices once got into their mouths, they very well employed their mouths. He had but one eye, but they called him blind cobbler, blind Hewson, and did throw old shoes and old slippers and turnip tops, brickbats and stones and tiles at him and his soldiers. He marched through the City to the Royal Exchange, where he stayed a little space. Then he marched to Guildhall, where he met with many affronts by the way, so that among the rude multitude there were some did fire a pistol at the soldiers and some that threw great stones at the soldiers, that did very much kindle wrath, that at last they fired in earnest, and four or five of the apprentices and others, whereof one was a cobbler, were killed and others wounded, and some likewise of the army very dangerously wounded . . .

Source C
(*The Declaration of Breda, 1660.*)

Charles, by the Grace of God, King of England, Scotland, France and Ireland, Defender of the Faith, &c., to all our loving subjects, of what degree or quality soever, greeting . . .

. . . to the end that the fear of punishment may not engage any, conscious to themselves of what is passed, to a perseverance in guilt for the future, by opposing the quiet and happiness of their country in the restoration both of king, peers and people to their just, ancient and fundamental rights, we do by these presents declare, that we do grant a free and general pardon, which we are ready upon demands to pass under our Great Seal of England, to all our subjects, of what degree or quality soever . . . (excepting only such persons as shall hereafter be excepted by Parliament). Those only excepted, let all our loving subjects, how faulty soever, rely upon the word of a king, solemnly given by this present Declaration, that no crime whatsoever committed against us or our royal father before the publication of this shall ever rise in judgement or be brought in question against any of them to the lease endamagement of them either in their lives, liberties or estates, or (as far forth as lies in our power) so much as to the prejudice of their reputations by any reproach or term of distinction from the rest of our best subjects, we desiring and ordaining that henceforward all notes of discord, separation and difference of parties be utterly abolished among all our subjects, whom we invite and conjure to a perfect union among themselves, under our protection, for the resettlement of our just rights and theirs in a free Parliament, by which, upon the word of a king, we will be advised.

And because the passion and uncharitableness of the times have produced several opinions in religion, . . . we do declare a liberty to tender consciences, and that no man shall be disquieted or called in question for differences of opinion in matter of religion which do not disturb the peace of the kingdom; and that we shall be ready to consent to such an act or parliament as, upon mature deliberation, shall be offered to us, for the full granting that indulgence.

And because, in the continued distractions of so many years and so many and great revolutions, many grants and purchases of estates have been made, to and by many officers, soldiers and others, who are now possessed of the same, and who may be liable to actions at law upon several titles, we are likewise willing that all such differences, and all things relating to such grants, sales and purchases, shall be determined in Parliament, which can best provide for the just satisfaction of all men who are concerned.

And we do further declare, that we will be ready to consent to any Act or Acts of parliament to the purposes aforesaid, and for the full satisfaction of all arrears due to the officers and soldiers of the army under the command of General Monck, and that they shall be received into our service upon as good pay and conditions as they now enjoy.

Given under our Sign Manual and Privy Signet, at our Court at Breda, this 4/14 day of April, 1660, in the twelfth year of our reign.

1 Study Source A. What reasons does Monck give for marching south. Please quote from the source when answering the question.

2 Study Source B.
  a) In your own words explain the situation in London in November 1659.
  b) How does this source help the historian understand the causes of the Restoration?

3 Study Source C.
  a) List the five main points of the Declaration of Breda. Use quotes to back up your selections.
  b) Why would those who had in the past opposed the Restoration of the Crown be reassured by the Declaration of Breda?

How to answer these questions
Read Chapter 10

Question 1
You need not only to quote from the source but also to explain the phrases 'the liberty . . . of parliament' and 'arbitrary and tyrannical usurpations'. (Monck is here referring to military interference with Parliament and the Committee of Safety.)

Question 2
- You must explain how public order was breaking down, the tax strike and the unpopularity of the Committee of Safety.
- You must point out that the source illustrates the unpopularity of the army and the slide into anarchy that made many wish for stable government.

Question 3
- You must look carefully at the Declaration of Breda. The main points are liberty of conscience; a free pardon to all who had opposed Charles I and Charles II; the question of ownership of ex-Royalist land to be settled by Parliament; Monck's

troops to be paid and taken into the King's service; and Charles to rule with Parliament.

- You must point our that the Declaration was aimed directly at those who might have fears about Restoration, not at Royalists whom Charles did not have to satisfy.

BIBLIOGRAPHY

Ashton, R. *The English Civil War: Conservatism and Revolution 1603–49*, 2nd ed. (Phoenix Giant, 1997)

Aylmer, G. *The Interregnum: The Quest for Settlement, 1646–60* (Macmillan, 1974)

Aylmer, G. *The Levellers in the English Revolution* (Thames & Hudson, 1975)

Aylmer, G. *Rebellion or Revolution? England from Civil War to Restoration* (Oxford University Press, 1987)

Baker, A. *A Battlefield Atlas of the English Civil War* (Ian Allan, 1986)

Barnard, T. *The English Republic* (Longman, 1997)

Bennett, M. *The Civil Wars 1637–53* (Sutton, 1998)

Carlton, C. *Going to the Wars: The Experience of the English Civil Wars, 1638–51* (Routledge, 1993)

Coward, B. *The Stuart Age: A History of England 1603–1714* (Longman, 1980)

Coward, B. *Oliver Cromwell* (Longman, 1991)

Cust, R. (ed.) *The English Civil War* (Arnold, 1997)

Fletcher, A. *The Outbreak of the English Civil War* (New York University Press, 1981)

Hill, C. *The World Turned Upside Down: Radical Ideas during the English Revolution* (Viking Press, 1972)

Hill, C. *Puritanism and Revolution: Studies in the Interpretation of the English Revolution of the 17th century* (St Martin's Press, 1997)

Hirst, D. *Authority and Conflict, England 1603–58* (Harvard University Press, 1986)

Holmes, R. *War Walks 2: From the Battle of Hastings to the Blitz* (chapter on Naseby) (BBC, 1997)

Howat, G. M. D. *Stuart and Cromwellian Foreign Policy* (A & C Black, 1974)

Hutton, R. *The Restoration: A Political and Religious History of England and Wales, 1658–67* (Oxford University Press, 1993)

Jones, J. R. *Britain and Europe in the 17th Century* (Arnold, 1966)

Jones, J. R. *Country and Court* (first chapter on Restoration) (Arnold, 1978)

Jones, J. R. *The Anglo Dutch Wars of the 17th Century* (Longman, 1996)

Kenyon, J. P. *The Stuart Constitution 1603–88* (Cambridge University Press, 1986)

Lynch, M. *The Interregnum 1649–60* (Hodder & Stoughton, 1994)

Morrill, J. *The Revolt of the Provinces* (Allen & Unwin, 1976)

Morrill, J. (ed.) *Reactions to the English Civil War 1642–9* (Macmillan, 1982)

Parry, R. H. (ed.) *The English Civil War and After 1642–58* (University of California Press, 1992)

Richardson, R. C. *Images of Oliver Cromwell* (Manchester University Press, 1993)

Roots, I. *The Great Rebellion 1642–60* (Batsford, 1981)

Russell, C. *The Origins of the English Civil War* (Macmillan, 1973)

Russell, C. *The Causes of the English Civil War* (Oxford University Press, 1990)

Russell, C. *The Fall of the British Monarchies 1637–42* (Oxford University Press, 1995)

Smith, D. *Oliver Cromwell* (Cambridge University Press, 1991)

Tomlinson, H. and Gregg, D. *Politics, Religion and Society in Revolutionary England 1640–60* (Macmillan, 1989)

Underdown, D. *Pride's Purge: Politics in the Puritan Revolution* (Allen & Unwin, 1985)

Wedgwood, C. V. *The King's Peace 1637–41* (Penguin, 1958)

Wedgwood, C. V. *The King's War 1641–47* (Penguin, 1958)

Wedgwood, C. V. *The Trial of Charles I* (Penguin, 1983)

Woolrych, A. *Soldiers and Statesmen* (Clarendon, 1987)

Woolrych, A. *Commonwealth to Protectorate* (Phoenix, 2000)

Worden, B. (ed.) *Stuart England* (Phaidon, 1986)

Young, P. *Civil War in England* (Longman, 1981)

INDEX